have a butcher's

the making of
lock, stock and two
smoking barrels

stephen marcus

with photographs by tim maurice-jones

The
History
Press

Front–cover image: © Universal.

First published 2017

The History Press
The Mill, Brimscombe Port
Stroud, Gloucestershire, GL5 2QG
www.thehistorypress.co.uk

© Stephen Marcus, 2017

British Library Cataloguing in Publication Data.
A catalogue record for this book is available from the British Library.

ISBN 978 0 7509 6793 8

Typesetting and origination by The History Press
Printed and bound by CPI Group (UK) Ltd

contents

Introduction

introduction

Life is interesting. It sends you lots of curve balls – some little, some huge. Some change your life completely and some just make you change course for a little while. I'm not sure what the curve balls in my life have done for me, to be honest. I do know that *Lock, Stock and Two Smoking Barrels* has thrown some pretty big curve balls into the lives of most of its cast and, of course, those of Guy Ritchie and Matthew Vaughn. Guy Ritchie wrote and directed *Lock, Stock* – he's now a top Hollywood director working with the likes of Robert Downey Jr and Jude Law. Prior to *Lock, Stock and Two Smoking Barrels* he was directing music videos. Matthew Vaughn, the producer, is now a Hollywood producer and director who launched Daniel Craig to stardom in *Layer Cake* and brought us *Kick Ass*, *Kingsman* and *X-Men*. Jason Statham was a market trader when Guy put him into *Lock, Stock and Two Smoking Barrels* and then into *Snatch*. From there he hasn't looked back, and is now a total Hollywood action hero (as if you didn't know). Dexter Fletcher, child star, is now a top director and writer. Nick Moran is a director and writer. Jason Flemyng and Vinnie Jones have both carved out Hollywood acting careers. As for me, I've gone onto work in Hollywood and the UK with Kate Winslet, Michael Caine and Joaquin Phoenix in *Quills*. Bill Paxton called me from his car while driving down the Pacific Coast Highway to offer me the part of Ted Ray in *The Greatest Game Ever Played*, opposite Stephen Dillane (*Game of Thrones*) and Shia LaBeouf.

Lock, Stock has allowed me to create and guide a walking tour. It's called The Gangster London Tour and it's a tour around the East End of London, taking in the sights and sounds of the gangster world (in that area mainly the Kray twins, with a few others thrown in) and gangster-related film locations, including several locations from *Lock, Stock and Two Smoking Barrels*. I get all sorts of people on the tour, from fans of the Krays and fans of the films to people who just love tours. I occasionally get a stag do, and it was on one of these stag tours that I had a bunch of Australians who had all come over for their mate's wedding. Being huge fans of *Lock, Stock* they thought a tour with Nick The Greek would be a good way to start the stag weekend. There was one lone English guy in the group, and during the walk we got talking. At the end of the tour he told me he worked for The History Press, and asked if I would be interested in writing a book about my experiences with *Lock, Stock*. I considered it for a few days and initially thought that having only worked on it for six days' actual shooting I might not have much to say. Then I thought, why don't I get in touch with the others involved in it and add in some of their stories as well? At least that way it'd be bigger than a church pamphlet.

That part of the introduction was written nearly two years ago. The book is now finished. I have got contributions and anecdotes from Jason Flemyng, Nick Moran, Vas Blackwood, Frank Harper, Nicholas Rowe, Steven Mackintosh, P.H. Moriarty, sound operator Simon Hayes and director of photography Tim Maurice-Jones. Tim has also given me some great photographs – Polaroids from the set, which head up each chapter. *Lock, Stock* was one of the last films to be shot on film, and Tim took Polaroid photos of nearly every set-up so that he could be sure of his lighting. During pre-production for the film, Tim and Guy met up on loads of occasions to discuss the shots. After each meeting, Tim would go away and meet with Peter Wignall and together they drew up the storyboard for each shot. Peter and Tim have let me use some of those images in the book (some original and some kindly redrawn by Peter). Thanks very much, chaps.

I have tried to get together with Guy and Matthew to get their stories – after all, it is their film – but due to schedules it hasn't been possible. Maybe we'll get together in the future and there'll be an updated version available.

thanks to

Tim Maurice-Jones for his contribution and the Polaroids.

Peter Wignall for all the storyboard images he drew.

Rory Gilder at Incentive Images for all his press images.

To all the contributors: **Nick Moran**, **Jason Flemyng**, **P.H. Moriarty**, **Frank Harper**, **Tim Maurice-Jones**, **Nicholas Rowe**, **Steven Mackintosh**, **Vas Blackwood**.

To my editor, **Mark Beynon**, for suggesting this book in the first place.

To my wife, **Sarah Nelson**, for her constant support in everything I do.

To **the fans** for just being fans of one of the best movies in British gangster movie history.

And of course thank you to **Guy Ritchie** and **Matthew Vaughn** for creating this film in the first place and giving me and many others a huge boost to our careers.

foreword
by paul tanter

Paul Tanter is a British director, writer and producer. He's been making films since 2008, his list of credits include Jack Falls, The Rise & Fall of a White Collar Hooligan, The Fall of the Essex Boys *and* Kill Ratio. *When I asked around for filmmakers to give me their thoughts on* Lock, Stock and Two Smoking Barrels, *Paul Tanter sent the reply below. I thought it would be a good foreword. Thanks, Paul.*

I first saw *Lock, Stock* during its initial cinema release in 1998. British film had been a rather mixed bag of late, but I always endeavoured to see the new releases in the cinema rather than wait for video. Sometimes this meant something enjoyable but a bit bland like *Shooting Fish*, and sometimes it was edgy new stuff like *Final Cut*. I was already aware of *Lock, Stock* due to a slightly naff ITV London news piece several months earlier about a gangster film featuring Vinnie Jones – one of those 'shooting now' reports. I've always wondered if they ever actually translate into publicity as they are likely forgotten by the time the film is out. Anyway, being a Wimbledon fan, the segment piqued my interest for the novelty value. As much as I loved Vinnie for his performance on the pitch, I figured his talents wouldn't extend to the big screen. How wrong I was.

A group of friends and I piled into the local Odeon in Putney, excited to see something that wouldn't be about a group of poverty-line northerners overcoming adversity to put on a performance of some kind. I realise now that *Brassed Off*, *Up 'n' Under* and *The Full Monty* were in the minority back then, but at the time to us it felt like they were very much the zeitgeist. Even *Trainspotting*, as cool as it was, wasn't exactly a feel-good film. I remember being excited by the Ska Films logo and crunchy guitar riff. It was slightly reassuring that the production company indicated quality with its cool logo and theme! You needed a few seconds to adjust to the very sepia tone of the film, but Jason Statham had us hooked straight away with his cockney sales patter, trying to flog his dodgy gold chains for a tenner each while Nick Moran roused the crowd up into digging their hands into their pockets. A terrific chase sequence with the boys and police overlaid with (yet more) crunchy guitars banging out 'Hundred Mile High City' by Ocean Colour Scene had us excited from the start.

Coming out of the screen and heading to the pub, we couldn't wait to excitedly dissect the film. Usually a film would get a cursory discussion before moving on to other things, but this one kept us discussing, debating and quoting all night. From the music ('All solid, even the Robbie Williams song was catchy.'), to the cast ('Haven't seen Hatchet Harry in much since *The Long Good Friday*'…'Vinnie Jones was great!') and the locations ('That was definitely Putney Bridge in that last scene with Jason Flemyng!' – It wasn't). It had captured our imaginations and several of us went back the next day to watch it again. This was the first time in my life I'd gone back to a cinema to watch a film a second time.

The perfectly cast ensemble of actors was a mixture of new talent and some familiar faces from various films and TV I was a fan of. Dexter Fletcher was arguably the biggest name amongst the four lads, while P.H. Moriarty was a good link to possibly the best British gangster movie ever made, *The Long Good Friday*. Then there were the ones we knew of but didn't know their names at the time: 'It's young Sherlock Homes!' (Nicholas Rowe); 'It's Bear Strangler McGee from the 'Gunmen of the Apocalypse' episode of *Red Dwarf*!' (Stephen Marcus); 'It's Danny John-Jules!' (We all knew Cat from *Red Dwarf*); 'It's that guy with the *really* throaty voice from the beginning of *Face*' (Steve Sweeney). I will admit that at the time I had absolutely no idea who Lenny McLean was, but I read up about him in the days that followed as I researched the film. The casting of the film is flawless. The four main guys have a perfect chemistry with each other, while every single support, especially Vas Blackwood, Frank Harper and Stephen Marcus, is just so right for his or her role.

The look of the film was and remains one of its defining characteristics. Guy Ritchie plays out many sequences almost like a music video: the card game and drinking session look and feel incredibly exciting. It was a style that many filmmakers would try to emulate in the following years, yet the only person who has ever bettered it is Ritchie himself in his subsequent works – *Snatch*, *Revolver* and *Sherlock Holmes* all being examples where he's continued to work this magic with this visual style.

I bought the soundtrack as soon as it was out and got the video on the day of release. Yes, video. The film was also on DVD, as I recall, but this is when DVD was about a fiver more than the video, and I was working at Tesco to fund my upcoming university course. I was to subsequently upgrade a year or two later once I had caught up with everyone else in the technical transfer to DVD, but for now it was video; and it got watched a lot. It was *Lock, Stock* that persuaded me and my friend Alec that we should pursue the idea we'd always had of trying to make a film, so he purchased a second-hand camera and we commenced. Everything we shot was terrible and thankfully none of it survives to this day, but you gotta start somewhere, right? Once I finally made the full switch to DVD, *Lock, Stock* was one of the first I got – for the extras as much as the film, special features still being something of a novelty then. It's one I still watch regularly, and it stands up today as strong as it did at the time. It has such a unique look that nothing about it has particularly dated. You could play out the same story today with no problem. Repeated viewings allow you to appreciate the nuances of the film – the varied but effortlessly cool soundtrack, Alan Ford's wonderful voiceover, Rob Brydon's comedic turn as the Traffic Warden – all easy to gloss over on first showing. *Lock, Stock* regularly and justifiably turns up in 'top ten' lists of British films and/or gangster films, and is currently #143 in the IMDB top 250. It stands now as a British classic alongside *Get Carter* and *The Long Good Friday*.

As a British filmmaker, particularly one who's made his fair share of gangster films, *Lock, Stock* has undoubtedly been an influence on me. Whilst it may have been followed by some attempted clones and copies, there's no doubt that it inspired a generation of filmmakers and reignited the gangster genre in the UK. Some critics would lazily accuse anything involving a voiceover or freeze frames as being a Guy Ritchie copy, forgetting these have been cinema staples for decades and notable in other crime films of the '90s, such as *Goodfellas*. Whilst Tarantino was already influencing films with pop culture references and emphasis on cool and funny dialogue, suddenly in the UK we had our own guy (no pun intended) to fly the flag for us. What was doubly great was that he followed it up with *Snatch*, proving he wasn't a one-hit wonder or a one-trick pony. As well as the flashy editing and cool sequences, there are some lessons for filmmakers in how to do things on a budget. Take for example the end shootout: it's vicious, and exciting … and you don't see any of it beyond the very first shot fired from Plank. The rest of it plays out off screen, through great sound design, breaking windows, and reactions from Frank Harper and Steven Mackintosh. Now there's a way to save yourself the time and expense of shooting an intricate gunfight between eight people in a tight space. The aftermath, in which Jason Flemyng walks through the 'pile of corpses', is suitably bloody and broken to match what we earlier heard and think we saw. I know Guy Ritchie storyboarded the whole film, so I assume this wasn't done on the fly when they were running out of time. It's just a canny and creative way to do something when perhaps the budget doesn't stretch far enough to enable you to do the all-singing, all-dancing version. Considering the budget was so relatively low that they had to get the first assistant director to play the Samoan pub barman, the Director of Photography to be drowned by Barry The Baptist (Lenny McLean) and even producer Matthew Vaughn to be carjacked by Dog (Frank Harper), the film still punches way above its weight in terms of production value. Its influence on popular culture was felt for years to come, with the mod look designed for the characters by costume designer Stephanie Collie making a big comeback over the following decade as the male audience chased down the same look as their on-screen heroes.

When I was casting for my first feature as a director, the producer and I went on something of a mission to get some *Lock, Stock* cast members involved, and it was a privilege to work with Dexter Fletcher, Jason Flemyng and Alan Ford on *Jack Falls*. We managed to last about four seconds with each before telling them how much we loved *Lock, Stock* and then asking them a variety of questions that I'm sure they'd answered a million times before (and with Jason and Alan this extended to *Snatch* too). I've since had the pleasure of working with Vas Blackwood several times, and I hope one day to work with Stephen Marcus, Nick Moran, Frank Harper, Vinnie Jones and Jason Statham. *Lock, Stock* definitely taught me the value of a talented ensemble with good chemistry, something I made sure we had on projects like *The Rise & Fall of a White Collar Hooligan* and *Essex Boys Retribution*. As someone who is often working on a budget, scenes like Big Chris caving in Dog's head with the car door, or the aforementioned shoot-out, showed me the value in violence sometimes taking place off screen rather than always having to show it on camera.

I'm still thankful to the film now, not just for the entertainment over the years but for inspiring me and a generation of other filmmakers to follow our dreams of making something just as entertaining.

'dunno tom, seems expensive'

Tom sells Nick a stereo.

Ed arrives at Tom's shop.

Ed, Tom and Nick walk through the shop.

Nick The Greek and Tom do a deal.

Tom gets money out of the oven.

BRIGHTON ROCK	1947
THE ITALIAN JOB	1969
PERFORMANCE	1970
GET CARTER	1971
VILLAIN	1971
THE LONG GOOD FRIDAY	1979
SCUM	1979
MCVICAR	1980
THE KRAYS	1990

As the list above shows, British gangster films have been around for years. These are some of them that came before *Lock, Stock and Two Smoking Barrels*, and below is a list of some that have come since. Some good, some bad and some great. We all have different opinions on which is which.

SEXY BEAST	2000
GANGSTER NO.1	2000
SNATCH	2000
LOVE, HONOUR & OBEY	2000
ESSEX BOYS	2000
LAYER CAKE	2004
THE BUSINESS	2005
RISE OF THE FOOTSOLDIER	2007
IN BRUGES	2008
BONDED BY BLOOD	2010

Lock, Stock and Two Smoking Barrels was released in 1998 by Polygram after almost three years of hard work by Guy Ritchie and Matthew Vaughn: three years of meetings, script writing and rewriting and rewriting and more rewriting, fundraising, pre-production, hunting down locations, putting together the crew and, of course, casting.

Guy Ritchie was introduced to Matthew Vaughn in 1995 through a friend of Guy's. Matthew had told the friend that he was a producer, so first-time director Guy exaggerated a few things about himself and a partnership began. Guy sent Matthew a copy of *Lock, Stock and Two Smoking Barrels* and Matthew took Guy's script down to the country and read it:

It had no ending and no real structure but it was a diamond. It had so much energy and was strong, funny, clever, new and original.[1]

MATTHEW VAUGHN

A few days later Matthew called him up. Guy acted some of the scenes over the phone to him and Matthew was convinced, 'Let's make this film.'

For two years they worked tirelessly on getting the film made. The whole process was made harder by the fact that Guy was a first-time film director; investors are wary of funding untried talent. The whole process brought them both close together and they built a strong friendship based on honesty and taking no bullshit from each other and the others involved in the film. For example, if you allow them to, a film crew can take forever to set up a scene and get going. The director of photography may take a long time lighting it, the art director may take forever dressing the scene, and of course the actors will stand around talking forever if allowed. When

---

1 Interview published in *The Independent* by Veronica Blake.

this happened Guy was often heard counting down from ten. When this was heard everyone would get going because nobody wanted him to get down to one. I never saw what happened if he did get to one.

The first draft that Guy wrote was 250 pages long. The powers that be say a page of script equals roughly a minute of film, so this film would have run at four and a half hours. Guy and Matthew spent the first two months polishing the script and trimming it down. Once the script was sorted, it was down to Matthew to get it financed. He punted it around all over the place and the script ended up on Trudie Styler's desk.

> I found myself laughing rather a lot ... I don't believe in putting money into projects. Having said that, I thought I'd take a punt on this one because I thought it was really worth putting some money into this one.[2]

TRUDIE STYLER

I personally remember some investors from Italy. Vas Blackwood (Rory Breaker) and I met them at Ealing Studios when we were in there for a fitting. People invest in films for many reasons, but often one of them is that they like to meet and hang out with filmmakers and actors. Being at the studios at the same time as the investors is a golden opportunity to impress them. But I guess we weren't that impressive, because they later pulled their money out, almost collapsing the production. How do they feel now?' wonders Vas Blackwood.

---

2   *The Making of Lock, Stock and Two Smoking Barrels*, Momentum Pictures.

It started out at £3 million and I thought, 'This is going to be *Lawrence of Arabia*, with big shots and panoramic stuff.' Then the budget got cut and cut, it ended up being less than a million. I shoot commercials with bigger budgets than that – in fact back then I was doing music videos with bigger budgets. Back then I'd do a Bjork video for a million. This budget was £800,000. Guy was like 'Can we do it for this money?' [I replied] 'I can do it for that, I'm used to doing it for cheap.'

TIM MAURICE-JONES

Tim Maurice-Jones was the director of photography and he got involved in the film because of working on music videos. Guy Ritchie saw a video that Tim had worked on for Take That, called 'Babe'. He called Tim in for a meeting and after a chat – and Tim thinking, 'I'm going to have to cut corners to make this work' – Guy asked him to do it. And Tim did cut corners; in fact he sunk nearly all of his fee back into the film to pay for the lights that he wanted.

Just as we were about to shoot there was a wobble. Some money had pulled out and there was a real sense of 'this might not happen'. There were days to go. That's when Trudie and Sting got involved, I think. I had a connection there. I'd worked with them on a film, *The Grotesque*, which Trudie produced. So when I heard there had been this wobble, I was like '*no*'. Then I got a call: it was all back on again. Matthew had done something and pulled something out of the bag.

STEVEN MACKINTOSH

We had all the money. We were at Ealing Studios. I was walking around the art department and they were printing up money and making half a ton of ganja, putting all the things together. I was shown around the studio space, 'this is where we're going to do this', and then suddenly, *bang*, they pulled out. It was all off and Matt was, 'Don't worry, I've got some tricks up my sleeve' … and he did and we were all back on. But then it was decided that he was going to use some sort of dodgy, hooky money, some gangsters' money. So Matt was, 'We'll, restructure, cut the budget and don't do it as a studio, do it all on location, tell everyone they're getting paid the square root of fuck all. I'll give everybody a bonus when it stands.' Handmade were supposed to be working as the sales agent. They had very little to do with the film, but they were the sales agent. They went bust a week into filming. Suddenly Matt had nothing – no sales agent, no distribution. He managed to borrow the money, a bit from Trudie (Styler), a bit from Peter Morton, a bit from Stephen Marks, a bit from a handful of his mates – total of about a hundred grand, but he kept it moving. He actually made a sort of socialist cooperative movie out of a bunch of arch Tories and aristocrats.

NICK MORAN

The budget dropped from around £3 million to about £800,000, and, as Nick says, everybody ended up working for low fees and part deferments – meaning we got half of our fees during working and half when the film was released and in profit. Now, most films don't go into profit, and you rarely see any deferred money. By that I mean that there is some creative accounting done so it looks like films haven't made profit. If they didn't really make profit, then who would be stupid enough to invest in them? *Lock, Stock* did go into profit, it made approximately $25 million and Matthew Vaughn and Guy Ritchie are two very happy bunnies these days. Matthew is a very loyal person and as far as I know everybody got paid the full deferments as agreed.

> I've never known a producer drive it through and turn it around: you've lost the money, you've lost the names, you've lost the sales agent, your route to market, lost the studio, everything – but he still made it. We've got 20 quid but we're still making it. Incredible. It went from £3 million to £800,000. When I got the phone call I was the lead in a £3 million movie to be shot in Ealing Studios, and I ended up in a £800,000 movie being shot on the back streets of Bethnal Green. God bless 'em. I stuck by them but they stuck by me, even more importantly.

NICK MORAN

I personally became involved with the film at the casting stage, obviously. I got a call from my agent, and he sent me a script. He's no longer my agent, as he let me go just before *Lock, Stock* was released – doh! My career shifted after it was released, and my new agent reaped the rewards. Anyway, the call said I had to read the script, and then if I liked it I had an audition with the casting director, Celestia Fox, and the director, Guy Ritchie. The script was a small, low-budget British movie called *Lock, Stock and Two Smoking Barrels* (a mouthful of a title).

When I read a script I find it hard to decide if it's good or not, even though I've read hundreds, and *Lock, Stock* was no exception. I couldn't tell if it was good or not. The dialogue was great but it jumped around and I found that difficult to follow. The characters were very exciting and funny, and I could see myself playing a few of them – that is what swung it for me, and I went for the audition.

People often ask if I knew that it was going to be a success; to be honest, I had no idea. You can never tell if a film is going to be a hit. There are so many factors: what genres are on trend? What are the other films being released at the same time? And, of course, is it actually a well-written and well-made film?

Lock, Stock broke the trends of all the gangster films before it (and created a few trends after it). Every twenty years or so a great British gangster movie gets released, and it was time for another when *Lock, Stock* came along. The audience took it to heart and they loved it, I think they loved the characters, the dialogue and, of course, the story.

Usually when I get an audition booked, I check up on the director. But this new fella, Guy Ritchie, had no track record except for a few music videos, adverts and a little short film called *The Hard Case*. This was the precursor to *Lock, Stock*. It's about a gambler in a card game – sound familiar? It stars Benedick Bates and Wale Ojo, and was written and directed by Guy Ritchie. So when I got the call for the audition I had no idea what to expect, and I also had no idea what role I was to read for. I don't think they did either. I went to a large house on Clapham Common, which was Celestia's office. I got shown into the waiting room where other actors were waiting, including Lenny McLean.

I didn't have a clue who Lenny was at that time – he was just another large actor, probably going for the same role as me. He quietly stood in the corner of the room, going through his lines. I didn't take much notice of him apart from his size. I thought I was a big unit, but he was huge. Not long after I arrived he got called down to audition. The audition room was down in the basement of this huge Clapham townhouse, so I couldn't hear anything coming from the room. Sometimes the waiting room is right next to the audition room, with only a thin wall between them. Not being able to hear someone else's audition is a good thing, as I can be put off if I hear what I consider to be a great audition. (It also works the other way and if I hear a pants audition then that can boost my confidence.) About ten minutes later Lenny came out of the room with an explosion of noise. His audition must have gone well. He'd gone from being this quiet brooding giant in the waiting room to Mr Loud Cockney Geezer, joking and laughing with everybody, which is the Lenny everyone knows and loves. Very quickly he was gone and the waiting room was quiet again. I didn't think about Lenny again after that until pre-production.

Now it was my turn. I was taken downstairs by a casting assistant (whose name I've forgotten, sorry) and into a very busy room. By busy I mean that the walls were lined with shelves of books and the floor was strewn with papers and scripts. The shelves included the set of books that every casting director has on their shelves, *The Spotlight Casting Directory* – an encyclopaedia of actors and actresses in the UK who have all paid to be in it in the hope that their headshot will stand out and get them the starring role in the latest hit film/TV show/theatre show. There was a chair set up in front of a small video camera and a couch behind the camera where Guy was sitting with Celestia Fox. I was introduced to Guy. I already knew Celestia from various other castings. I don't really recall the audition itself, because, like most actors, I go to an audition, give it my best shot and then leave and forget about it until I get a call telling me that I've got the job. I do remember that Guy wasn't horrible or unpleasant and the audition was a nice experience. There was another person in the audition room reading in lines for other people.

> **I got a call and they were doing casting, they asked me if I would sit in and do the readings for the other actors they were auditioning. I had no idea if I was up for a role. I liked the script so I said yes.[3]**

DEXTER FLETCHER

I didn't actually audition for Nick The Greek, I auditioned for Tom, the role played by Jason Flemyng, and I did a screen test for that role. I've never seen that screen test, so I'm not sure whether I did well or not. I guess I did ok, because I got a part in the film. I think we did the scene near the start of the film where the four heroes are in Soap's kitchen gathering all the money for the poker game. The purpose of the screen test in this case was not to test our acting skills but to see how the four actors worked together and to see what chemistry there was between them. I guess the chemistry didn't quite work for me as I got a call a few weeks later telling me I'd got the gig but Guy wanted to offer me the role of Nick The Greek and not Tom. Obviously I agreed and took the role. It was a great part. Guy actually gave himself a credit as a casting director; and rightly so – after all, he cast Jason Statham, Vinnie Jones and Nick Moran.

There were a lot of people who auditioned for roles they didn't end up playing, or were on the cast list in the early stages but didn't end up on screen: Ray Winstone was

---

3 *The Making of Lock, Stock and Two Smoking Barrels*, Momentum Pictures.

originally cast to play Barry The Baptist. There was a picture of Ray on the wall in the production office at Ealing Studios with the middle of his head shaved off and a comb over with great big '70s-style glasses on.

Barry The Baptist would be Big Vern from *Vis* magazine.

NICK MORAN

Jude Law was going to play Winston, and Tom Hollander, Mark Addy, Terence Stamp and Albert Finney were also cast, but because filming kept getting put back and financing kept changing a lot of the agents pulled their clients off it.

Nick was very lucky. Once they'd cast him Guy and Matt stuck by him even though many other people weren't sure. The idea was to cast this unknown who gave a great screen test and surround him with great named actors like Albert Finney and Terence Stamp. Nick didn't get it straight away; he had to wait for a few people to turn it down.

I remember Guy saying, 'I'll tell you now, that's the best screen test we've done. That was brilliant, that. But it's all about names and faces in this game so ... good luck, son.' He walked me to the door and said goodbye.

Everybody had to turn it down – Ethan Hawke, Stephen Dorf ... there was a series of actors who turned it down. I remember, I didn't even get the audition through the agent. I got an audition because a friend of mine, a very good actor called Rocky Marshall, went in for an audition. Guy was very forthright with him and said 'I'm looking for people who are a bit more modelly.' The actors he was getting he just wasn't really feeling. I'd just signed with Select Model Agency to subsidise my erratic acting career and Rocky said 'you should

see my mate, he's just signed with Select. We done a couple of films together.' That's what got me in the door and then I did four other screen tests after that.

I remember sitting in the park trying to get a tan and doing chin ups. I was thinking 'I've got a recall, I've got a recall, I've got to get buff and tanned for this recall.' So I'm sitting in the middle of Stockwell Park trying to get brown, you know tiny bit of sunlight, and I'm chasing this little bit of sun around the park. So I went into the recall looking slightly brown and buff. I get the phone call just before one of the festivals – not Glastonbury but around that time – and I'm running around whatever festival it was like a madman shouting 'I've got this film.' So that's June, July, and then we're actually on the cobbles in November, December. We finished just a couple of days before my birthday in mid-December.

NICK MORAN

Casting director Celestia Fox said on the first day of filming that this film would be a massive flop with Nick Moran in the lead. The first day we shot Ed arriving at the gym for the card game.

They were all behind the monitor, including Celestia. She was convinced I was going to get fired in the first week, and had this other fella waiting. I did it and showed them I know what I'm doing. Give Celestia her due, she apologised and admitted she was wrong to me, and to Guy and Matt, and phoned up my agent and apologised: 'I made a terrible mistake, I was mistaken. This guy is going to be a star and if not he'll have a wonderful career.'

NICK MORAN

Like me, Frank Harper and Nicholas Rowe auditioned for different roles. Nick originally auditioned for the role of Winston but lost out to Steven Mackintosh.

I originally went in and read for one of the four boys parts. Looking back on it now, that was probably the biggest chunk of dialogue. I forgot all about it and then I got a phone call saying the film's going ahead and the script's on its way, and they've offered the part of Dog. I thought 'What the fuck's that?' The script came and I read it, and I thought 'Fuck me that's one of the biggest parts in the film, that's a result.'

FRANK HARPER

I was sent the script. It was one of those where they were sending you a script with a view to you coming in for a meeting. I read it. I immediately loved it; it just kind of flew by. I just thought it was smart and funny, and there were lots of great characters. I met Guy at Celestia Fox's office in Clapham. I can't remember if maybe I read for some different character. I have a memory that there was another character in the gang who in a later draft ended up gone from the story. I think I read for that character, who got absorbed into the other four as rewrites were done, and I think I also read for Winston. It was one of those, 'have a read of both'. I remember coming away thinking, 'This script is such fun, I'd really love to do it', and then I got the call saying, 'They'd really love you to be involved; they're still figuring out which role you be right for.' So there was that discussion and also the film not fully financed yet. It wasn't ready to go. This must have been a year before it went. I remember being attached to it for quite a long time. Then I get a call, 'The gang member you read for isn't going to exist anymore but they'd really

like you to play Winston.' I was like, 'Yeah, great, I'd love to do it.'
But they weren't ready to go so it was one of those cross fingers
and hope it gets made because I'd really love to do it. I remember
waiting and waiting, and occasionally checking in with my agent –
'any news?' – and then eventually …

I had a great year in '97. I shot a film called *Land Girls* at the start
of the year in Dorset and went straight on to do *Our Mutual Friend*
for the BBC, and it was while on that I got a call saying it was ready
to go and they were going to shoot at the end of the year. I just
remember what an amazing way [it was] to finish off this great year.

STEVEN MACKINTOSH

I asked to play Winston, but they said 'it's already cast', so when
it came around and we got the offer I just thought it was such a
brilliant script that I didn't care what I did. I just wanted to be in it.'

I lost out to Jason Flemyng, as I said, because Guy and Matt really
wanted him on the film because he had some heat about him at
the time. He'd done the lead in a film called *Alive and Kicking* with
Anthony Sher in which he played a young gay ballet dancer.

NICHOLAS ROWE

Guy was casting the film about a year before it got made, and I
went into the casting with him and Celestia Fox. He was looking for
the real McCoy, which he got with Lenny and a few of the others.
So I went in there and faked it. Even though I'm a south London
boy, I've lived an easy life, and so I pretended to be the real McCoy.
And then it collapsed. Matt Vaughn being the producer was trying
to keep everybody that he had together and had organised these
socials. I realised that if I turned up to these being me then Guy
would soon suss that I wasn't the real McCoy, so I kept avoiding

them, and then when I turned up on set I'd just finished doing *Tess of the D'Urbervilles*. I turned up with black hair and sideburns, and they were like, 'What the fuck is that?' After we'd got a few days under our belt and they had realised I was this over-privileged south London boy it was too late.

JASON FLEMYNG

The great thing about Jason being cast as Tom was that the part was originally written for a fat bloke and he was called 'Fat Tom' a lot, but the genius of Guy Ritchie is in his casting decisions and the confidence to follow them through. So, when tall and skinny Jason Flemyng was cast instead of big and fat Stephen Marcus, rather than cut all the references to him being fat he kept them in. When we were filming at the shop for the opening scene after a short discussion the gags about skinny Jason being fat were born.

P.H. Moriarty was cast as Hatchett Harry. P.H. is one of those British actors who crops up every now and then in great British films such as *The Long Good Friday*, which also starred Bob Hoskins. It came out in 1980. It's about a gangster who's getting involved with the development of London's docklands when somebody is muscling in on his action. P.H. plays his right-hand man, Razors. It's a fantastic film and I recommend everyone to watch it. An interesting side note is that it's Pierce Brosnan's first film. He plays an IRA hitman. Not all of P.H.'s film have been great, however. He did star alongside Dennis Quaid in *Jaws 3-D*, which got five nominations in the 1984 Razzie Awards: Worst New Star, Worst Picture, Worst Supporting Actor, Worst Director and Worst Screenplay. Fortunately he was fantastic in *Lock, Stock*. He's the only actor I've known who can scare the crap out of you while wielding

a black rubber cock. His involvement came through Vinnie
Jones. They met at a charity golf day down near Cardiff.

> I said to Vinnie, 'Been seeing a lot of you this year in your game.'
> He said, 'Oh yeah. You support Wimbledon?' I said, 'No, Millwall.'
> My friend and I, when Millwall are away, we go and see a premier
> division team, and because they're quite local to us we used to go
> and see Wimbledon down at Selhurst Park. So what happened was,
> he said, 'Next time, after the game I'll leave some tickets out for
> you to the bar, our private bar.' He ran it. He said, 'No one can go in
> there unless they've got these tickets, see.' Me and my friend we had
> seats in a director's box, a good director's box, right at the top with
> a good view. So we went in there and he said, 'You didn't pick your
> tickets up for the bar. How'd you get in?' I said, 'Excuse me, I know
> who you are, you don't really know who I am.' 'Yeah, I know you're
> an actor.' He said he liked me in *Good Friday* [*The Long Good Friday*].
> I said, 'The guys on the door know who I am … either I can come in
> or I can't.' He said, 'Oh, yeah, ok, but I like to keep control.' Even the
> away players had to have tickets. It was his bar. So I was in there one
> day, and he says, 'I've got these two public school boys want to meet
> you. I'm playing this guy in this film, and they want you to play this
> character. They'll be here in a couple of home games' time.' So they
> come down and I meet them; they're Guy and Matthew. They start
> telling me about this film, and this character, and I says, 'Have you
> got the money for the film?' Matthew said, 'No, but we will get it.' I
> said, 'Great. When you got it, let us know.'

P.H. MORIARTY

They got the money, they called him, and P.H. was one of the
first actors on set in November 1997.

Simon 'Purple' Hayes was the sound mixer on the set. He has a very good story of how he got involved:

Me and Guy were going to the same clubs and the same parties when we were about 14 or 15 years old. Guy was hanging around with a load of blokes from Fulham and Putney, and I was hanging around with a load of blokes from Sheen and Richmond. My group of blokes and Guy's group would be in clubs and parties up the King's Road, trying to blag Chelsea girls, so there was a bit of rivalry between our two groups. When I met Guy I think he was living in Fulham. One of his very good friends, Alex De Rakoff, was in my school (funnily enough he's now directing a TV series of *Snatch*). My very good friend, Albert, had a fight with Guy in Kensington Pool Club, which was downstairs underneath Kensington Market, in about 1984 or '85. The fight involved pool cues being broken over each other's heads. When Guy was a teenager he had a lot of energy and he was well known around south-west London, as we all were.

The first time I came across Guy in the film game was when I was working on a commercial. I was about 24 years old. I saw this runner and I kind of recognised him. I hadn't seen Guy for a few years. I was trying to work out where I knew him from and he was trying to do the same. He sidled over and we put two and two together and realised how we knew each other from the clubs etc. As I said, he was running, and I said, 'What do you want to do?' And he said, 'I wanna direct.' I said, 'Listen mate, every runner wants to be a director. Why don't you set your sights a little lower and try being a clapper loader?' He said, 'Bollocks, I wanna be a director.' I remember his confidence back then and he was determined to be a director. I was doing very well out of doing commercials, but what I really wanted to do was mix sound on dramas, so at the weekends I would go and shoot people's shorts. So Guy says that he's managed to get hold of some 'short ends' [bits of film stock that hadn't been used and had been re-canned and stored in a production company's fridge] and he's going to shoot a short. I said, 'I'm in,' straight away. This was 1995.

We shot the short over a weekend in Soho, and it was called *The Hard Case*. It was clear right from the outset that Guy absolutely should be a director, because he had balls the size of watermelons; he had no problem at all getting his point across, he had a very visual eye and he could tell his heads of department exactly what he liked and what he didn't. His best skill was working with the actors. He understood what he wanted and he understood how to make the best of an actor's own character and build that into the character he wanted in his script. So we shot it and had a great time, and I went up to Guy on the Sunday and thanked him and he thanked me for doing it for fuck all. He said he'd had such a great time on it that he wasn't going back to running and he was going to direct commercials and music videos, and that he was going to get funding to make the full version of the short. Driving home after with Arthur, the boom operator, who was new to the business and hadn't heard all the BS that goes on, he said, 'This is great – we're going to do a feature with that fella.' I said, 'Arthur, they all say that. Everyone is going to make a film and they never do mate. Don't hold your breath.'

Two years later, end of 1997, I get a phone call out of the blue. It's Guy and he says, 'We're going to do it.' 'Do what?' 'The film. I've got the money and I've met a producer and we're going to do it. We're going to make the film. I've written the full script; I want you to read it and do the film. We've got the money; not loads …' As soon as he said that I started thinking deferment, and I started that swerve conversation that I use when I don't want to do something. But he cut me off and said, 'Read the script that's coming over by bike courier this afternoon and let me know.' As soon as I heard the words 'bike courier' I knew he was serious, because you don't use bikes if you've got no money.

SIMON HAYES

'they lack any kind of criminal credibility'

Nick brings Tom the guns.

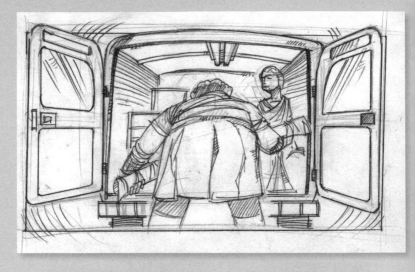

Nick gets the guns out of his van.

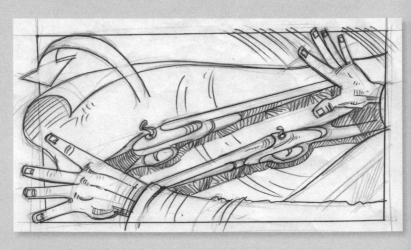

The guns are revealed.

Tom is concerned.

Nick reassures Tom.

Pre-production

This, for an actor, can mean a few things. While everybody else is running around like crazy, building sets, doing deals, searching for locations, fitting costumes etc., the actors are being fitted for costumes, having discussions about hair and, depending on the type of film, getting fitted for prosthetics. On some films you may be lucky enough to get a bit of rehearsal.

I did a couple of films for the Wachowskis, *Speed Racer* and *Ninja Assassin*. I rehearsed on both of them. For *Speed Racer* it wasn't rehearsal in the true sense. I was called out to Berlin two weeks before shooting, which I thought was odd because I was only doing a couple of scenes with a kid and a chimp. They wanted me to get to know the chimp, so I spent those two weeks staying in a fancy hotel in the centre of Berlin and rehearsing – having a good time playing with Kenzie the chimp everyday. What I didn't know at the time was that I had developed a gum infection that had given me halitosis and nobody told me, so there's a great picture of me holding Kenzie and he's got his hand over my mouth, stopping the smell.

On *Ninja Assassin* I had to do a big fight with the lead, Korean pop star Rain. We rehearsed for a couple of weeks and then shot the fight over three days. I played a character called Kingpin, based on the Kingpin character in Spiderman. The scene involved me being stabbed, punched and kicked, and then finally having my head smashed into a urinal – not the first time I've ended up with my head down a toilet!

For *Lock, Stock*, Guy had called me up and asked me to try a slight Greek accent, so as part of my own personal rehearsal I got together with a Greek Cypriot friend of mine, Chris Loizou, at the Groucho Club in Dean Street, Soho. After a few vodkas we went through every word, and together we got to what I thought was a pretty good Greek accent. Unfortunately, when I got into rehearsal with Guy he didn't think it worked, and we cut it. His actual words were 'Forget it, you sound like Stavros.' Stavros was a comedy kebab shop owner created by Harry Enfield in the 1990s. Although I stopped using the accent, I think that I had worked on it so much that a little of it stayed with me, because I'm always being asked if I'm Greek. Sorry if you think I'm Greek but I'm not – I was born in Portsmouth.

In making this film I am trying to create something that is credible and relatively humorous. Comedy and gangsters are inseparable, the truer the villain, the funnier they are, that is not to say it is necessarily Ha! Ha! Funny. I found that I was continually having to rein in the comedy elements so that it didn't become too farcical.[1]

GUY RITCHIE

I'm guessing that's why he cut my accent. Nobody else seems to remember the rehearsals, so maybe I was the only one – maybe Guy looked at me and thought 'this one needs help'.

I don't remember doing any rehearsals, I do remember going to Ealing Studios for costume and make-up tests, and I had the black hair and sideburns, and they said, 'We'll just shave your head.' And that's how I ended up with that look. You know that scene later when we're all getting drunk and celebrating, and Statham sticks a

---

1   www.filmscouts.com

£20 note in his mouth and lights it like a cigar? You'll see I'm wearing a beanie hat. That's because it was shot nine months later and I was doing another film and my hair had grown and I couldn't cut it.

JASON FLEMYNG

I didn't do any rehearsals, but I was at costume and I was talking to Guy, and he said, 'I want you to be more London.' So I said to him, 'How can I be more London, Guy?' This went on for a while and he got the casting lady in (Celestia Fox) and she said, 'Well, he is a Londoner?' I said, 'What you talking about, being a right cockney?' so one day I went, 'Hello Guy, ahs it going mate? Awrigh?' No one talks like that. He went, 'No, I don't want that. That's too much.' So this went on for two weeks. I couldn't work it out and he couldn't explain it. So I'm on set and queuing up for breakfast and I said to the guy 'more bacon' and I heard this voice – 'more London'. Guy is standing right behind me. 'Fuck me, Guy. Let me have something to eat first.' He was good-humoured, I like Guy. Then I suddenly realised what he wanted – 'wan'ed'. He wanted the 'th' dropped out of words; instead of 'through' he wanted 'frew'. So I said, 'I think I know what you want, you don't want the right grammar [I think he means articulation here]. The accent's alright, it's a London accent, you don't want the grammar.' I said, 'Like, people say hose. You want 'ose, like an O. You're quite happy with that then?' He said, 'Keep speaking like the way you said, otherwise you're going to start throwing in all the 'th's and stuff.' He was good-humoured about it. So that's how we got that compromise in the end.

P.H. MORIARTY

It wasn't a rehearsal. When you're doing a split screen phone call you have to have the timing down or you're not reacting to each other correctly. I think what we did was record the conversation and then you mimed it or had the other end of the call played back to you, otherwise the timing would be off. They might say something and you may start to answer before they finish.

TIM MAURICE-JONES

Nick Moran has a story that demonstrates Guy's understanding of the world he's created and of the characters that are populating this world, and also about his awareness of his personal limitations and budgetary limitations.

There's a brilliant element of originality about *Lock, Stock*. It's well produced it and it's well directed. That's something people don't necessarily get their heads around. When you direct a film it's always as if you're in a fight, and Guy, he sort of adapted everything so it's like, 'Fuck this, let's make it funny. That's still entertaining. Because we haven't the money to make an amazing car chase.' The rest of it had warmth and charm and humour. If someone ad-libbed a funny line, if I came up with something funny or Dexter or Flemyng, he'd be like, 'Right, let's have that.' The best example is the traffic warden scene, which everybody loves. The original scene was written as:

'Right, Bacon, see what we've got.'

'We've got loads of weed, a bag of cash and a traffic warden.'

'What are we doing with a traffic warden?'

'I don't know. Let's dump him at the lights.'

That's what it was meant to be. Then Guy said, 'I can't believe this. I've got forty minutes to do this one shot and we're gonna have time left over. Let's improvise something.' The camera was locked off and we drove round and improvised.

I said, 'Don't touch him up, knock him out,' and Guy fell about. He went, like, 'That's really funny but you can't say that.'

'What?'

'No, no. You're not the funny one. Jason [Flemyng] says that, that's funny. Jason says that cause that's funny. He's the funny one.'

'Oh, for fuck sake,' and then I went, 'I fucking hate traffic wardens,' and we climbed over the back.

That was my impro, and everyone looked at the monitor and fell about. That's one of many classic moments in that film and it was completely improvised. Guy let people improvise because it was like, 'What have I got, I haven't got all the money, I haven't the stars or a leading man anyone has heard of but what they do bring is this freedom and frisson, and that's just as entertaining as something that's flash and got all the money.'

NICK MORAN

Wardrobe

Once you've been offered a part and done the deal, but before you've signed the contract, the first person to contact you is normally the costume designer. They want to know your measurements so they can start getting everything together. Stephanie Collie was our designer. 'Designer' doesn't necessarily mean that he/she designs the clothes from scratch. It means that they work closely with the director to help achieve the style that the director is looking for and also with the director of photography to make sure the costumes don't clash with his lighting design. The colours of the costumes can severely change the lighting set-up, or sometimes, as happened to me once, the director of photography just has an aversion to a colour. This guy I worked with hated the colour green and nobody was allowed to wear green on set – so much so that he sent home a crew member because he wore green to work one day. I wore a green shirt one day – not intentionally, honest – but because I was a cast member he couldn't do anything about it, and all through the blocking, before getting into costume, he was visibly squirming every time he looked at my green shirt.

The budget for *Lock, Stock* was quite low, so Stephanie didn't have a great deal to work with, and as you may have noticed I'm a big fella and my clothes are not bought in the usual places. We met up to go shopping at High & Mighty in Edgware Road, London, my go-to store for all shoots – and for my own clothes. We got a few suits from there, but we never used them. Probably because delays in the shoot dates meant they had to be returned while she could still get a refund on stuff. Often on low-budget films they buy stuff and then return it after the shoot. I've had to cut a few shots because a label has got stuck in my arse. They can't return them if the labels have been removed. At one point I was called into the production office at Ealing Studios for a fitting. It was here that I met Vas Blackwood for the first time. Vas is a very funny fella and an amazing talent, very confident. When he is in a room everybody follows his lead, and this I think comes across in his performance as Rory Breaker. We didn't really talk much that day, but we both noticed on the wall of the office the photographs of all the cast, including Ray Winstone in the role of Barry The Baptist – the role that Lenny McLean played. Ray's photo wasn't an ordinary actor's headshot, it had been doctored and showed him with glasses and a shaved head – not a full shave, but down the middle, like he was balding. Ray never did the role. This was most likely because of contractual obligations on another film that came up first because of the delays on *Lock, Stock*. It doesn't seem to have affected his career much.

The original cast changed massively. When I was at Ealing, Ray Winstone was attached, and Jude Law, Tom Hollander, Mark Addy. They all had pictures on the wall. And then word went round that they didn't have any money, and Guy was very upset because a lot of the agents pulled the plug and ran away. I remember talking to Ray Winstone and he was, 'Nah, it's never gonna happen that film, never gonna happen.'

NICK MORAN

At some point Matthew Vaughn did a deal with French Connection UK – partially due to Nick Moran and Jason Statham, who have both modelled for FCUK. And partially thanks to Trudie Styler's friendship with Stephen Marks, owner of FCUK. Stephen is listed as executive producer on *Lock, Stock and Two Smoking Barrels* and has gone on to executive produce on many of Matthew Vaughn's films. I was once at Cannes Film Festival, not long after *Lock, Stock*, at a party with some of my mates, when the producer Stephen Wooley came up to me and started pitching a film idea. I thought, 'This is great. My life has changed. He wants to make this film with me in it.' But as he was telling me this story, I started to realise that there was no role in it that sounded like me. When he finished, he asked me what I thought. I looked at him and said, 'Who do you think I am?' He replied, 'Stephen Marks.' I corrected him, he apologised and we said goodbye. There have been a couple of occasions where people thought I was Stephen Marks. Anyway, FCUK ended up fitting out the four heroes with some designer suits. And then this meant that we all had to be more sharply dressed.

I was taken to a costume supplier named Carlo Manzi, and after a rummage through his rows and rows of costumes we very quickly realised that he wouldn't be able to fit me, so I was measured for a tailor-made suit. I wear the same suit throughout the film, a nice pale-blue two-piece number with a subtle check, which when the filming was done was returned to Carlo's stores for use by me (and others) in future productions. The poor suit finally met its demise on a music video for my mates Brandon Block and Gee Moore, AKA GB United. The song was called 'Zeus Dance', a club song based around the Greek music used as my theme in *Lock, Stock*. That track was originally used in a film called *Zorba the Greek* starring Anthony Quinn, and is called 'Zorba's Dance'. It was written by Mikis Theodorakis. The video shoot was quite hard on the suit. It was shot in a very hot Cyprus and involved me riding around on a scooter, dancing knee-deep in mud and chasing Brandon and Gee around Aya Napa and the surrounding area. Sadly this resulted in the suit getting the arse ripped out of it halfway through the shoot, and all shots after that had to be carefully framed to avoid my naked arse appearing. After all nobody wants to see *that* bouncing around. That's why I've never done porn. (Although I was asked once; I said no.) The suit was binned after that.

Keep It Together

One of the first things Guy and Matt did as part of pre-production was to organise various social events to keep everyone together and help bond the groups. These drinking sessions for the boys, dinners round his house and poker nights continued on set. Matthew was a very good poker player and often took the boys for substantial amounts of money. The irony is that Nick Moran plays Eddie, a great card player, but Nick is crap and regularly lost to Matthew, as did Jason Flemyng.

> We played three-card brag. Matt was not a rich man at that time and he used to play this game. He was good. So good that we did some reshoots, three days, and I had to do them for free because I lost so much money to him.

JASON FLEMYNG

Another event was a five-a-side football tournament. It happened about two or three weeks before the first day of principal photography and was held at Spitalfields Market.

Spitalfields is a covered market just inside the City of London. There has been a market selling fruit 'n' veg on the site since 1638. It has now moved to New Spitalfields Market in Leyton. Some people say the market has been there since the thirteenth century, but officially the market began in 1638, under King Charles, to feed the new London boroughs of Whitechapel and Bethnal Green, where *Lock, Stock and Two Smoking Barrels* was predominantly shot. When the market moved to Leyton in 1991 it became a very popular fashion, food, arts and crafts, and general market, open seven days a week. It's very busy at weekends now, but when we were preparing for *Lock, Stock* it wasn't so busy, and they had some small footy pitches in the middle of it.

I may have imagined this, but I think everybody was divided into the groups that they would be in the film and they were pretty much like this:

The Four Boys:
Ed (Nick Moran), Bacon (Jason Statham), Tom (Jason Flemyng), Soap (Dexter Fletcher) and JD (Sting)

The Villains:
Barry The Baptist (Lenny McLean), Big Chris (Vinnie Jones), Hatchett Harry (P.H. Moriarty) (he didn't play), Little Chris (Peter McNicholl)

Dog's Gang:
Dog (Frank Harper), Plank (Steve Sweeney), Paul (Huggy Leaver), Mickey (Ronnie Fox) and John (Tony McMahon)

Me and others:
Nick The Greek (Stephen Marcus), Rory Breaker (Vas Blackwood), Nathan (Elwin David), Traffic Warden (Rob Brydon)

Posh dealers:
Winston (Steven Mackintosh), J (Nicholas Rowe), Charles (Nick Marcq), Willie (Charles Forbes)

The other actors and crew made up the numbers.

For some reason Robbie Williams turned up and played that day. I don't know if he was just passing or if he was invited, but he proved a welcome addition to the day because, as you may know, he is a skilled and keen footballer. Robbie is one of the forces behind Soccer Aid, along with his best friend Jonathan Wilkes.

I have no memory of who won the tournament. However, I do remember having the ball at one moment and I looked up to see Vinnie Jones and Lenny McLean charging towards me. I know I'm a big fella but Vinnie isn't exactly small and Lenny was a man mountain. I look into their eyes and I just see two of the hardest men in Britain with 'death, kill, death' in their eyes. I imagine the feeling a zebra has when it sees a couple of lions bearing down on it is similar: 'This is it, my life is over. I am about to be eaten.' My only thought was, 'Get rid of the ball.' I passed the ball to Vas, and he hoofed it up field. I'm not a coward but I'm not stupid either. We lost that game.

I was there! That was just before we started at Spitalfields, which looked so different then. I remember having a drink in that bar and then watching this football match, which was being shot, and Robbie Williams was there. He was being filmed playing football, and I remember thinking, 'I can't quite get my head round this.' There was talk of this being part of the title sequence and I thought, 'How is this going to work with the rest of the film?'

STEVEN MACKINTOSH

All I remember is being terrified. I didn't want to be opposite Vinnie, I wanted to be on Vinnie's team. I think I played on Robbie Williams team. Why was he there? I'm just sorry they didn't use any of that stuff because I put my life on the line for that. They filmed it. They were going to use it in the opening titles or something. He just had this notion that he might do that. I don't know how that would work and clearly it didn't because they didn't use it.

NICHOLAS ROWE

3

'if you hold back anything, I'll kill ya'

Rory Breaker.

CUT TO:

NICK: "ERR."

CUT TO: CAMERA TRACKS WITH RORY.
RORY WALKS FROM BEHIND
DESK.
RORY: " DON'T FUCKING ERR
ME GREEK BOY! HOW IS
IT THAT YOUR SO FUCKING
STUPID ... ETC ... "

Filming began in November 1997. Things are a little unclear as to which was the first scene shot. Maurice-Jones says:

> The first scene we shot was at Borough market with Jason Statham selling the moody goods. Jason had done a lot of that before so he knew what he was doing. He'd also been a model and an Olympic diver.

TIM MAURICE-JONES (director of photography)

However, Nick Moran says:

> The first scenes were in the boxing ring, walking in and the card game. Nearly a week doing that. So I was already a week in and seasoned before everyone else got on set. That was at Repton Boxing Club, everything was at Repton except the doorway, which was just a doorway in Bacon Street or Brick Lane because the set-up at Repton didn't work for us.

NICK MORAN

Yet Simon Hayes says:

> I can remember when Jason Statham turned up on his first day and Jason Flemyng, who has been an actor his whole life, said to him, 'When this fella (pointing to the focus puller) puts his marks down, you've got to hit those marks because if you don't hit the marks you're going to be out of focus and anything you've done you're going to have to go and do again.' Statham turns to the focus puller and says, 'I don't know what it is you're doing, but if I'm doing something you don't like, you let me know and I'll sort it out.' He was completely open that he didn't know what people on the film

crew were doing, but he was also open to being told and adjusting his technical performance. This resulted in his confidence growing and growing throughout the shoot, so that when it came to the opening scene he went to Guy and said, 'I've heard that you've been thinking about this opening scene. I used to sell stuff on Oxford Street and I've written some dialogue.' That dialogue was his own patter from when he was on Oxford Street. Guy said, 'We'll shoot it; if it works we'll stick it in.' It worked.

SIMON HAYES

If Statham's confidence grew throughout the shoot, then that couldn't have been the first scene shot, as Tim suggested. Time plays havoc with the memory.

There's a myth that Guy saw Jason doing his patter on a street corner and said to himself, 'He's got to be in my film.' Unfortunately, that is all it is: a myth. It would be fantastic if it were true. It is the fantasy of a lot of people to be recognised on the street and be turned into a film star, and it does happen on occasion, but not in this case. Jason auditioned the same as everybody else, as far as I know.

So, the first week's filming was most likely at Repton Boxing Club in Cheshire Street, Bethnal Green. A little history of the club is needed here, because it is a very influential part of Bethnal Green. It was originally built in 1884 by the Repton School in Derbyshire as a way to help the poor kids in the poorest part of the East End. Local boxers and boxers from miles around come here to train and emulate the champions who have come out of this place. As well as training fighters, it helps to stop a lot of kids going into crime.

Around here, there are two things for a working-class kid to do: steal or box.

TONY BURNS (head coach at Repton)

The club has been coached by Tony Burns forever, it seems, and he's trained many champions there: John H. Stracey, Olympic gold medallist Audley Harrison, and former middleweight world champions Maurice Hope and Darren Barker. Also, actor Ray Winstone trained here. He was going to be a boxer, before he discovered acting, and he was very good. As a Repton boy he won eighty out of eighty-eight fights. If he'd played the role of Barry The Baptist he could have relived his youthful glories in the ring.

As well professionals, a lot of the more colourful characters from the East End have trained here, including Ronnie and Reggie Kray and Mad Frankie Fraser. The Kray Twins weren't bad boxers; they weren't great, but they weren't bad.[1] Reggie was the schoolboy champion of Hackney and went on to win the London Schoolboys Amateur Boxing Championships, as well as being a finalist in the Schoolboy Championships of Great Britain. In 1949 he became the South Eastern Divisional Youth Club Champion and the London ATC Champion. Ronnie was also the schoolboy champion of Hackney, and won the London Junior Championships and a London ATC title. Charlie Kray said this about his brothers:

1   http://boxrec.com/media/index.php/Reg_Kray

As boxers, the Twins were quite different from each other. Reggie was the cool, cautious one, with all the skills of a potential champion and, importantly, he always listened to advice. Ronnie was a good boxer too, and very brave. But he would never listen to advice. He was a very determined boy with a mind of his own. If he made up his mind to do something, he'd do it, no matter what, and unlike Reggie he would never hold back. He would go on and on until he dropped.[2]

CHARLIE KRAY

These longstanding gangster connections at Repton made it a perfect location for the card game run by Hatchett Harry.

A large part of the film was shot around Cheshire Street and just off it in Pedley Street where there is the most amazing set of arches that are used in many films and television dramas. You cross over the railway that runs into Liverpool Street station via the oldest railway footbridge in London and come down the other side into what is one of the moodiest places I've seen in London. It's very secluded, so it gets used for all sorts of late-night shenanigans and naughtiness. You have to watch where you put your feet when going down the steps because you can find human pee and poo, junkies' needles, used condoms, all sorts. When I first went there I was researching for my walking tour, and as I came round the corner at the bottom of the steps there were two cars parked with their boots open and something was being exchanged between them. It was very much like the film scene in which

---

2   http://boxrec.com/media/index.php/Reg_Kray

the boys have stolen the drugs and the van from Dog and his gang, and are swapping the large amount of ganja over to Tom's car to take it to Rory Breaker – so it is unsurprising that Guy chose this location to film it. He also used the steps on the bridge for the opening sequence where Bacon and Ed are being chased by the police and the case of stolen perfume bursts open, sending boxes tumbling over Ed.

Further down the road is the crossroads of Cheshire Street, Chilton Street and Grimsby Street, with the famous Blackmans on the corner. Blackmans is an old shoe store that has been there for donkey's years and is a Shoreditch institution. It's known as 'that plimsoll place' because you can get all kinds of plimsolls for a fiver. It has a great logo outside that reflects the comedic attitude of Phil Knight, who owns and runs it: 'The devil may wear Prada but the people wear plimsolls.'

The whole crossroads was converted into an imaginary porno empire belonging to Hatchet Harry, and Blackmans was the exterior of Harry's offices, where he beats the guy with a big black cock and the shoot-out takes place. The interior, where those scenes were shot, is at the old Bethnal Green town hall, which has now gone the way of many old buildings in London and been converted into luxury apartments. The sequence starts with Big Chris (Vinnie) bringing the antique flintlock rifles and the bag of money back to Harry at his office. He is watched by the two scousers, Gary and Dean (Victor McGuire and Jake Abraham). They go in after he leaves and then have a big shoot-out with Harry and Barry The Baptist (Lenny McLean). All four are killed. Our four heroes pull up and park outside a shop on the opposite corner to Blackmans. Ed and Tom go inside and find the money and the guns. They leave with them. Meanwhile

Pedley Street, then and now. This is where the two cars were swapping goods between them at the bottom of the steps and is also where Tom and the boys switch the drugs from Dog's van to their own.

This is the junction where the big sequence at the end of the film was shot. It's where Big Chris smashes Dog's head in with the car door.

Big Chris has returned to his car, parked up the street, to find Dog (Frank Harper) holding a knife to his son's throat. Dog wants some of the money so Big Chris drives them down to the office – 'It's a five-minute walk or a two-minute drive.' He drives his car into the back of our heroes' car and then does the scene that at the time caused a massive fuss – he pulls the unconscious Dog into the footwell of the car and begins to smash his head in with the car door.

This movie could have been salvaged morally by practising more restraint in its violence.

MOVIEGUIDE.ORG

… delivering the most terrifying portrayal of cockney screen villainy since Oliver Reed's Bill Sykes.

EMPIRE

The whole violence of the film and particularly this scene were likened to Tarantino. The fact is, though, that, unlike in Tarantino's films, in *Lock Stock* the violence and blood is only implied. You don't see any of it. In this scene all you see is an overhead shot and close ups of Vinnie Jones' face in violent fury. And at the end of the film when Rory Breaker's gang and Dog's gang all get killed, you only see a drop of blood through a cracked door and some windows getting blown out. You don't see blood spurts or bullets ripping bodies apart, and in this scene with Vinnie and Frank you don't see any heads being crushed like melons. I think Vinnie was particularly good in this sequence and so terrifying as he smashed poor old Dog's head.

For a while before filming began Vinnie had been having a row with a neighbour over access for the neighbour's horses across Vinnie's land. The day before Vinnie's first day on the film, he went out shooting birds in the woods – Vinnie loves to go clay pigeon shooting and hunting pheasants etc. He and Guy shared a few occasions doing that in the country after filming. After his day out shooting, Vinnie came home to find that the neighbour had pulled the contentious fence down and run his horses across Vinnie's fields. Vinnie wasn't happy and decided that a conversation was needed, so he went round to the neighbour's house and the conversation very quickly escalated into a row and then into a fight, during which Vinnie bit the neighbour on the forehead. The police were called and Vinnie was arrested, and because he had guns in his car he spent the night in a cell proving ownership of the guns and showing licences etc. He came directly from the police station to filming the next morning, went straight into make-up and then on set to shoot the sunbed scene.

I think Vinnie was using this incident as therapy and was picturing the face of the neighbour when he was smashing the car door into Dog's head!

Big Chris has a quiet word with Dog.

I've spent a small amount of time with Vinnie and never experienced his violent side, although I nearly did on one occasion. I lived in LA for about eighteen months and I was bored one day. My wife had gone back to England to sort out some details on our flat in Fulham, so I called up Vinnie and we arranged to play golf at Burbank Golf Club. He turned up with a little Mexican fella and they both looked a mess – they'd had a weekend of fun in Vegas. The golf course was beautiful and Vinnie and his mate were both very good golfers. We had a nice round and a few beers in the clubhouse after. At the end of that day I learnt a valuable lesson not to judge a book by its cover. I had assumed that Vinnie's Mexican friend was his gardener, and that Vinnie, being a nice guy, was treating him to a fun-packed weekend. When we left and he drove off in a gold Porsche, I discovered that he wasn't being treated, nor was he a gardener; he was part-owner of one of the big hotels on the Vegas strip. Vinnie then invited me up to his house that weekend for a barbeque, but I didn't go – I can't remember why. As it turned out, that was probably a good thing, because after the family afternoon Vinnie went down to the Château Marmont on sunset strip, where he got into a fight with Tamer Hassan. The two had a previous disagreement at Vinnie's house over Christmas, and when they tried to talk it out in the château the argument boiled over into a full-on fight. They're over it now and friends again.

For quite a while I was under the impression that the car scene was Vinnie's first day on set, but P.H. Moriarty (Hatchett Harry) tells me it wasn't. P.H. is an old-school actor, and when he and Vinnie got on set together P.H. Moriarty had a little piece of advice for the new boy:

We're on the set at the town hall and we're all set up for my close-up; Vinnie's my eye line. So, were all ready to go, and I look up and there's no Vinnie Jones. So I says, 'Where's Vinnie?'

The assistant director says, 'You don't need Vinnie. I'm doing it.'

I says, 'No, you're not. You're not tall enough.'

He says, 'Well, you'll have to do it.'

I take me microphone off.

Guy says, 'What's up?'

'If you want to do a professional film, get the right person to deliver the next line. I don't want it being read by him, someone who ain't even an actor. He can't get the feeling for it, Guy.'

So I went back to the trailer and I see Vinnie and he says, 'You packed up early.'

'I ain't packed up,' I said. 'You don't know, but when you're doing the eye line for somebody, you're acting with someone. No matter who you are, they stay there and deliver the lines, their lines to you. And when you got the reverse shot I'll do the same for you. I won't disappear. But you don't know, Vinnie, you wasn't told.'

Vinnie wasn't fazed by being the new boy.

So with that we went back and done the scene. I look up and he's got chewing gum under his eye and a big dildo. I struggle to keep a straight face. Anyway, I collapsed laughing.

P.H. MORIARTY

P.H. didn't get on too well with that assistant director. This story is from the first week of the shoot, at Repton Boxing Club:

You remember the guy at the table with the pony tail [Jimmy Flint]? It come to the day when we was doing the scene in the gym where I'm leaning on the ropes and Ed arrives. In he walks and I say, 'I suppose you're so and so's son' …

The dialogue actually goes like this:

Harry: Hello, you must be Eddie. JD's son.
Eddie: You must be Harry. I'm sorry I didn't know your father.
Harry: Never mind, son. You just might meet him if you carry on like that.

It's one of my favourite bits.

… So we was in the rehearsal after lunch and all the others come back and the assistant director starts into him [Jimmy]: 'Who do you think you are? Coming back fucking late, making people wait for you,' and he starts in with the poking. Jimmy tells him the runner's only just told him. The assistant director then gives him a shove and that's it, he cops a left hook and puts him on his arse. I loved it, absolutely loved it. The assistant director then started giving it all the, 'You'll never work again, you're out of here.' He tried to dig him out a few times after that too, and everybody thought this is out of order and they said so. So then he started getting me and Lenny on set half an hour before we was needed. So we had to put a stop to that. He used to send this runner down and we said 'this ain't right' so we told him to get the assistant down and he come down to the trailer and I pulled him inside and Lenny grabbed him and said 'Come here, son,' and sat him between us and said, 'Do you know why we called you here? It ain't for sex, it could be a bit painful, though.' We told him it was wrong getting us to set early, that he was disturbing us going through our lines. Anyway, he got upset by this and went to Guy and was going to leave. Guy saw the funny side, but he said 'He's right upset that kid and he's threatening to leave. We're not paying a lot of money, but we need these people.' So we explained to him we was only having a laugh.

P.H. MORIARTY

Although it was written and directed by a new boy, produced by a new boy, photographed by a new boy and introduced some new actors to the world, *Lock, Stock* also used some more established filmmakers.

New school has lots to offer, like tearing up the rule book.

I want this to be flash. Show off, be flash with the camera. Don't be worried by all the constraints you would normally have.

GUY RITCHIE to TIM MAURICE-JONES

When we all arrived on the set, as far as the technicians were concerned we were all at the top of our games. But the reason we were there was because none of us had any track record in feature films. We came together to make this film because the old school of features, they didn't want us in, because we were the MTV generation.

SIMON HAYES

And old school has its way of doing things, too; it's not always by the rules:

You remember the stunt man who gets run over by the mini? He doubles for Frank Harper as Dog. It was the funniest stunt I've ever come across. So, we're setting up and somebody says:

'Have you got any wires? How you going to do it?'

'I'm just going to let it hit me.'

'What do you mean you're just going to let it hit you?'

'As it comes close, I'll step onto the bumper and go over the top.'

'Have you got any pads?'

'No, I'll be fine.'

So we turn over, and the car comes shooting down the road and hits him. He goes flying over the top and lands in a heap in the road. He gets up, groaning, and asks how it was. Guy says, 'I need another one. Can you do another one?'

'Yeah, I think I've got one more in me.'

So we turn the car around and go again, and again it hits him and he lands in a heap. He slowly gets up, and I saw the massive bruise on him that went from his knee to his armpit. That's old-school stunt work. His only technique was to step onto the bumper and lift himself up a bit to roll over the car.

TIM MAURICE-JONES

Rory Breaker deals with Nick The Greek.

Football and Tabletops

My first day on set was in Clink Street on the south bank of the Thames, opposite the Clink Prison Museum, doing the scenes at Rory Breaker's office. It is, incidentally, the same street as the location for Bridget Jones's apartment in *Bridget Jones's Diary*. I arrived in the morning and was shown to my trailer – which sounds a lot more glamorous than it is in reality. On a big-budget Hollywood movie it would indeed be glamorous – a huge Winnebago filled with drinks, treats and a television. On a low-budget British movie like this it is one part of a three-way. A three-way is a big trailer divided into three changing rooms. There are usually changing facilities, a toilet and/or a shower, a desk and a sofa. Sometimes they come with a TV, but they rarely work. The walls are very thin and you can hear the person in the trailer next to you breaking wind (I feel sorry for those next to me), and when somebody gets on or off, the three-way rocks like a boat. When I get off it's more like a hurricane hits the boat. My costume was waiting for me in there. I changed into my suit and went to make-up, where Vas Blackwood was in the chair. We went over our lines and chatted a bit and then I returned to my trailer. I ended up sat in there for a couple of hours. This is why actors have trailers – because there is a lot of hanging around and waiting while things are being set up.

When I got to the set I found out why there had been such a long delay. Guy was in a foul mood. His day was not starting well. Part of the set was a bank of television screens that Rory is watching a football match on. The screens had arrived late, so they weren't ready to go in the morning when the cameras should have turned over. That was the first thing. The second thing was that when they finally got the screens up and running they couldn't show the planned Manchester United match because of a copyright issue. The screen guys had brought an American football match as an alternative. Guy is not a big fan of that sport, and even less now. But Rory Breaker is a London boy. He wouldn't be watching American football. The television guys didn't have any other tapes. A search went out for anybody with any football tapes handy, but with no success. The guys did have a tape of IndyCar racing, so that had to be used, even though it wasn't really in character.

It was a copyright issue because Sky Sports or whoever was controlling football wouldn't give us permission to show football and they gave Guy American football. He hates American football: 'I fuckin' hate American football, I fuckin' hate it.' He was furious because it was stopping work. I didn't let any of that get to me. I wasn't fuckin' about. I noticed that Guy was so much in the zone that I had something to do for him and I just couldn't get involved with the other hoo hah.

VAS BLACKWOOD

The other big thing that caused the delay was that while prepping the set one of the crew stepped back and accidentally put his foot through the top of the glass table that was to sit in the middle of the office. To get a replacement was going to take a few hours. A lot of people would have probably moved onto another scene while waiting, but not Guy. He came up with one of the greatest pieces of improvisation by a director I have ever come across, and one of the most memorable sequences in the film – the glass of orange juice being dropped through the tabletop by me. We shot the whole sequence in reverse, starting with Rory Breaker doing the 'I'll Kill Ya' speech. Vas did a brilliant piece of his own improvisation in this – he steps straight through the middle of the table. We nearly lost the first take because everybody was stifling laughter. It's very subtle in the film because it's framed so you don't see Vas's bottom half, but you can just see the movement as he lifts his leg over the metal frame of the table. His face doesn't give away anything, which makes it so much funnier. Then we shot the drink being brought in by Chopper and then finally, when the new glass top arrived, I dropped the drink through it.

> We were doing a line-up, which is where the actors show the crew the scene. So I'm standing there watching and Vas takes a step toward me, so I step back and I step back right into the central piece of the room, a large gangster-style glass coffee table. I thought, 'Fuck, this is it. I'm going to get fired. He's gonna go mad. He's either gonna fire me or chin me.' But Guy, cool as a cucumber, said, 'Don't worry about it, give me a moment and I'll come up with something.' Then he laughed and said, 'That was funny, I'm gonna nick that and put it in the scene.' And that's how the whole sequence came about.

SIMON HAYES

Stereos and Plastic Phones

The second day for me was shooting in a local corner shop in Hackney off Hackney Road. This was to be the shop belonging to Tom for the first scene in the film. This scene is a really good example of Guy's great scriptwriting and film-making: he sets up what the film is about, introduces the main character, sets up their relationship and sets up the style and language, all in one sequence. Tom gets his money; Soap has his, Bacon too. In this short sequence, we find out what they're doing, who they are and why they're doing it. All told by Alan Ford's voice over. Alan plays the barman at JD's bar and was of course Brick Top in *Snatch*. This also introduces us to Guy's style: short, crisp scenes with no unnecessary shots or words.

> **Guy has no attention span, which is why he's a great director. Films go by really quickly. Dyslexia is a big part of it; I'm dyslexic, Guy's dyslexic, Pete Wignall [camera operator] is dyslexic. I think because we've got a short attention span it makes the film really lean. There's no fat on *Lock, Stock*. Every single second means something. There's no long, lingering shots. There's just stuff happening.**

> **TIM MAURICE-JONES**

One of the first things that was discussed on that day was the fact that Jason Flemyng is not fat and there were several gags throughout the script about his character's fatness. If I remember correctly Guy wanted to cut the references to it, but Flemyng wanted to keep them in because it's funny that they joke about him being fat when he's not. Guy liked that idea, and it was decided that at every opportunity characters would refer to Tom being fat, so the scene opens with us talking about what he's been eating and is followed up by Soap referring to him in the next scene as 'the fat man'.

It's funny how time messes with your memory of things. Here are two memories of the same gag. I remember it the same way as Flemyng.

The point about Tom was he was meant to be fat and … Guy's talent is in his confidence and his sense to do what he instinctively feels is right. So he decided to cast skinny Jase as fat Tom, and it became a thing, which is one of the first things we did in that supermarket: 'You think you're fat but you're not fat.' 'I'm fucking skinny. Why do you keep calling me fat?' and that gag became part of the vernacular of the film, because that was what Guy thought was funny and he was right.

JASON FLEMYNG

Yeah, Flemyng was gonna do a different role, then Guy got the idea to write a gag in about losing all the weight and people still called him tubby Tommy and he's paranoid about his weight, you know how people lose lots of weight. It came about because Guy wanted Flemyng in the film as one of the boys. Flemyng desperately wanted my role, but Guy didn't see it like that, but then came up with the whole skinny fat guy thing.

NICK MORAN

One of the great things about Guy is his ability to spot a good opportunity to get a subtle laugh. He found, in the back room where we were 'haggling over £100', a comedy phone shaped like a packet of French fries and he just threw it into the scene. You forget about it until later, when you see me on the phone to Dean about the guns. The brilliance is that it is treated as totally normal that a super fence like Nick The Greek would use a French fries phone. Nobody takes the remotest bit of notice. I often get asked if I still have that phone: sorry, folks, but no, I don't.

The famous French fries phone.

Another bit of skilful directing and understanding of comedy is when I, Nick The Greek, pull out a massive wad of cash to pay for the stereo and the boys' reaction is, 'Jesus, Nick, you could choke a dozen donkeys on that. What do you do when you're not buying stereos, finance revolutions?' Then Tom brings out an equally large wad of cash and nobody says a word. Great writing, directing, delivery of lines and comic timing all combine to make us laugh and introduce the characters and their relationships. This scene also introduces us to the great use of language that Guy employs, with some classic lines that I am always having thrown at me by fans:

'Alright, keep your Alans on.'

'It's a deal, it's a steal, it's sale of the fucking century.'

I could write down lots more, but then I might as well just reprint the whole script, because nearly every line in every scene is a gem.

Bums and Guns

The arches in Pedley Street, off Vallance Road, Bethnal Green, was the location for Tom's garage/lockup where I bring him the guns so the boys can rob the neighbours of their stolen drugs and money. Sadly, those arches aren't there any more as they were pulled down in 2007 to make way for the new London Overground and Shoreditch High Street station, which is one of the reasons that Shoreditch is now hipster heaven. It's funny how places change. I went to drama school in Old Street, around the corner from Shoreditch. I used to get the no. 55 bus from my bedsit in Hackney through Hackney centre and Shoreditch to college nearly every day. I would look out the window and think, 'I wouldn't want to get off here.' Not because it was a bad area (although it wasn't great), but because there was nothing there but big old warehouse buildings and sweatshops for the fashion industry and the occasional strip club – most of which are still there. But now it's full of bars, restaurants and advertising agencies, and it's one of the trendiest places in the world. If you go down there on a weekend you'll find lots of Japanese fashion victims and Essex boys out on the lash.

I turned up on the day at the unit base. I got dressed and went through hair and make-up and then I was taken to the set. It was a hive of activity: the set being dressed by the art department, sound setting up (Arthur, the boom operator and Simon 'Purple' Hayes), Tim Maurice-Jones (director of photography) setting the camera and lights. And in a corner was a very nervous fella, who I later found out was Charles Bodycomb, the armourer in charge of looking after the two shotguns that I buy from Gary and Dean and pass on to Tom. I found out later that the reason he was nervous was that these guns were the real deal and worth around half a million quid. In fact several people were nervous that day. Not only were those guns worth a lot of money, they were also expensive to have on set, as Nick explained in this tale of another day on the shoot:

> That bit with, 'the British Empire was made on cups of tea', all that came about because the props guy didn't book the guns that day, so we didn't have the guns to walk in with and Guy's like, 'We haven't got the fucking guns?'
> The AD answered, 'They're not in the budget. They're expensive.'
> We stood around, and then I said, 'I'll just say, "I forgot 'em."'
> We had shot the scene that follows, when we had the guns, on a previous day.

> **NICK MORAN**

Those guns were a huge part of the film, on camera and off. They got their own theme music within the film, their own minder; the film is about the guns and the money.

When we came to rehearsing the scene, Guy walks me over to a red van and he tells me that's where I'm going to bring the guns from. He wants me to start bent over and to wiggle my bum a bit. It wasn't until I saw the film that I found out how close up to my bum the shot was and how large it looked. (Yes, I know I don't need to go on film to see how big my arse is.) A lot of actors like to look at the monitor to see how they're doing after a take. I don't, so I don't generally know what the final shot looks like. I figure the director knows what he's doing and if I'm going off track he'll tell me.

My arse has featured quite a lot in my career. My first film was *My Beautiful Laundrette* with Daniel Day-Lewis, in which I play Moose, a member of a racist gang. At one point in the film we harass a car full of Asians. Before the scene I jokingly said I was going to stick my bare arse in the window. Somehow this got to the director (Stephen Frears) and he made me do it. That was my introduction to filming. Never joke about what you're going to do unless you're willing to back it up. I've done it quite a few times since on other jobs. I'd probably be doing it now, if I hadn't done a little photo shoot for my old flatmate. The shoot involved me spending the whole day sitting between two very attractive bums that belonged to a hot neighbour and a hot lap dancer I knew. At the end of the day the girls then turned round and said, 'We've had our arses out all day. Now it's your turn,' so I had to do a picture for them. When I looked at the picture I was shocked and vowed never to get my arse out in public again. I've done really well in keeping to that vow – not.

Ray's Gonna Kill Sweeney

Steve Sweeney plays Plank. I want to share a couple of stories from Frank Harper about his behaviour on set. I couldn't find a way of fitting them into the stories so far, so I'm just putting them in here for your entertainment.

When Sweeney's on the money he's brilliant and he was brilliant in *Lock, Stock*. We was filming at the Borough (Dog's gang's office, which is now the office of fashion designer Paul Smith). Where it was on the corner is the Market Porter [pub]. It was just before Christmas. What we used to do was say to the drivers, 'Do you want to sit in traffic for an hour? Or have a drink and then drive home when the traffic has gone?' This time, I walk in the bar with Ronnie Fox, and Steve Sweeney's going up and down the bar singing 'Consider Yourself' from *Oliver!*

'Steve, what the fuck are you doing?'

'Call me Jack, call me Jack.'

'What?'

'Just call me Jack. The geezer who owns the pub thinks I'm Jack Wilde from *Oliver!* He keeps giving me free drinks.' And every now and then Sweeney would burst into songs from *Oliver!* and get free drinks.

There were times he wouldn't go home. I'd come into work and he's been in the pub till chucking out and then he's slept in the three-way. He did that for three days once.

Another one was the day that they had rigged the set for the machine gun. They put squibs [bullet hits] all over the set, and Guy was looking quite worried. Guy said to us, 'We can only afford to do this once. If you' – me and Sweeney – 'don't hit your marks, then we can't rebuild this thing and do it again. We can't afford it. We've only got one shot at this.' I said, 'Guy, you're talking to the wrong person. I can hit me marks, it's Sweeney you got to worry about. You better keep him out of the pub.' So we kept him in the three-way and out of the pub, and Sweeney stayed sober.

We was at an awards thing, somewhere in the West End and someone comes out the toilet: 'Ray's gonna kill Sweeney.' I go in there and I have to pull Ray off him. An hour later, Ray has to pull me off him.

You know when his head goes through the wall? So, they got this stunt guy in and he's saying, 'Look it's a really easy thing. Frank, you grab Steve, give him a shove, and, Steve, put your hands up to stop yourself before you hit the wall. 'Cos were going to cut away to your head going through the wall.'

Sweeney's like: 'Give it, Frank, go on. Do it Frank, give it. Do it hard Frank, do it hard. Go on, do it. Do it as hard as you like.'

Now I'm thinking 'Alright Steve, calm down.'

'No, Frank, go for it, go for it!'

So we do a couple of run throughs and I'm going at half-speed because the camera's not turning.

'What you doin'? Do it hard, Frank.'

'Steve, the camera's not turning. Wait till the camera's running and I'll do it hard. Don't you worry about that.'

So, anyway, we go for the first take and, boom, he don't put his hands up. He goes straight into the wall, half knocks himself out. He's now got another head growing. They're trying to get frozen peas off the caterers, and now he wants to fight me.

He done *EastEnders* and they gave him a driver. You don't get a driver on *EastEnders*. They done it to keep him in line. After three days, he's going home and he decides he wants to go to Ministry of Sound. He says he'll only be an hour. Well, he's in there all night, comes out and goes straight to set. He's walking around Albert Square, off his nut.

I love Sweeney. He's a great actor and great fun, but, in the words of Barry The Baptist, 'He's a fuckin' liability.'

FRANK HARPER

'he's got some adhesive mates'

Barry The Baptist.

Bacon sells the stolen goods.

The boys prepare to rob the neighbours.

Soap does some cooking.

Tom needs Nick's help.

When a film shoot comes to an end there's a little thing called a wrap party. It's a way of the producer saying thank you for everybody's hard work. Usually it's the last day of the shoot for obvious reasons – everyone gets hammered and is usually too hungover to work the next day.

Lock, Stock's party was at a basement bar in Greek Street, Soho; everyone I've asked doesn't know the name of it. I don't remember much about it myself except arriving and talking briefly with Lenny McLean and Vinnie Jones, and then I remember leaving and seeing Guy outside smoking a massive cigar. I spoke to him but he didn't answer – he just gazed off into the distance. He was probably very tired from the long six-week shoot and the whole party, and it was late by then. Or it may have been the large vodkas. I left after that and didn't see Guy until the premiere.

Nick Moran lived with a few mates in an old pub in Stockwell that was a squat. This pub became the centre of the film's late-night social events:

> It was a great place, I lived there for about five years but I began to feel like a benefit scrounger living in a squat with a vintage sports car outside, so I moved out. But it was great place to live with a bar and a band room downstairs with a recording studio. Everyone had a floor each, and there was a roof terrace and loads of spare rooms, which is why Statham used to stay over a lot during the shoot. I remember when Adam Bohling (production manager) crashed over one night. We'd been out and he'd got 'royal marines' drunk. I'd set an alarm clock for him and I went downstairs and he was still there with the alarm clock smashed to pieces all around him. I made a cup of tea and called him a cab before I woke him up:
>
> 'Adam, it's quarter to 8.'
>
> 'Fuck, fuck.'

'I've booked you a cab. Here's a cup of tea.'
'Fuck, I've got the keys to the location.'
I gave him his tea and off he went.

NICK MORAN

Adam was found the morning after the wrap party asleep in a skip outside Nick's squat. It didn't do him any harm, as he's gone on to produce loads of films with Matthew Vaughn: *Kick Ass*, *Kingsman*, *Layer Cake* and *Telstar: The Joe Meek Story*, which Nick Moran wrote and directed.

I used to get people drop by all the time after the shoot or whatever. There was this time when Tony McMahon had organised a night at EC1 for the cast and crew, and we all went. I wasn't drinking, I was behaving for the film, so after a while I thought 'I've had enough of this' and I got a cab home. Then out of nowhere everyone, and I mean everyone, turned up at my door, all the girls that were runners were there all shitfaced and my mate Dave, who I lived with, refused to believe I hadn't invited them. I'm standing in my pyjamas just going to bed and he thinks I invited them.

NICK MORAN

Nick tells the story of the wrap party and how the after party came to be at his pub:

It was all relatively civilised, a nice little venue in Soho, a few scuffles here and there. What do you expect with a cast like that? Their friends are bouncing about and there's a few interlopers that thought they could gatecrash, which ain't gonna work well. Not at that party. So there's a few people went home with their tails between their legs. They eventually throw us out at two in the morning, because of the scuffles, and everybody's milling about in the street, saying, 'Where we gonna go now?'

Flemyng's like, 'Why not have everyone back at yours?'

After a pause, I'm like, 'Yeah, why not?'

So in the middle of Greek Street I'm like, 'Everybody we're going to go to 36 ...... in Stockwell.'

Then I became like Bruce Forsyth: 'Did everyone hear that? This side of the street: we're going to 36 etc.,' and they chant it back to me. And then, 'How about this side of the street? ...'

So I end up with everyone in the street reciting the address, and then I tell 'em all to get in a taxi and off we go. Me and Flemyng jump into a cab and everybody turns up. The place was rammed. I was finding people in cupboards and shit a day later. I'd said to my housemates I was probably going to invite a couple of people back after, and I'd invited them to the wrap party. I'd laid in a couple of crates of beer just in case. It was madness. I think Richard Gere was there at one point. It was just insane. Everybody was there. They were upset that the bar had thrown out early at 2.00. They [the bar] were like, 'There's been some trouble. You all have to go.' It was really good end note, everybody back at this disused pub that was a squat.

So, you might think, now that the shoot has finished and the wrap party has happened, that the work is done. Not quite. At this point the work begins again for Guy and Matthew: post-production and sales.

For the director, post-production means editing, sound mixing, sound design, music, visual effects and picture grading. The actors and the crew are done when the filming wraps, unless they have to come back and do ADR (automatic dialogue replacement). This is when the actor has to come back and record dialogue that was recorded live on set but for some reason isn't useable or needs to be reworded. Guy didn't know what ADR was, and when Simon Hayes explained to him that it was getting actors in to dub their lines again, he said, 'What? Like some Kung Fu movie, where it's all out of sync? I ain't having that.' So between him and Simon they made sure that they got all the dialogue clean and clearly heard on set, so no ADR needed to be done.

Making a film is one of the most amazing experiences and the editing process is one of the best parts of it. It's where you get to realise what's been in your head for years.

> **Guy phoned me up and said, 'This is fucking blinding! We're in the West End, in the cutting room, this is going together lovely. You've got to come and look at some of the footage. There's people making us coffee, it's blinding.' So I went up to Soho, to Niven Howie's edit suite – [he was] the editor. Firstly because I wasn't doing anything, and secondly because the idea of hanging about with all these people I'd had such a blinding time with really appealed, and finally because I thought I might get a free sandwich.**
>
> **SIMON HAYES**

Actors and film crew are driven by the catering. The catering on the shoot was not thought too highly of by the crew. Because the shoot ran close to Christmas, the caterers put on a Christmas dinner during filming at Dorney Court for the old house robbery scenes. The entire crew boycotted the meal. The catering bus was laid out with decorations and trimmings but no one turned up. Well, no one except Adam Bohling, the location manager. Adam was an ex-marine and he hated to see food go to waste, plus he felt sorry for the caterers, so he was found sitting alone on the bus trying to eat all the Christmas food that the caterers put on; he made an impressive dent in the spread.

The four boys all stayed close and socialised like mad after the shoot was over. They would regularly go out and get seriously messed up, which did occasionally cause problems for the post-production process and got them into trouble with Guy.

I remember this time I was in Soho with Statham and I was shitfaced and my voice all scratched to fuck. I said, 'I've got to do the voice over with Guy in the morning, but it's alright it's only the guide track.'

I turn up at 10.00 in the morning and Guy's like, 'Fucking go home.'

'But it's only the guide.'

'But you're still fucking working. Go home.'

I didn't realise that as an actor you finish filming and that's when the fun starts, but as the director you're still working, doing the edit and the sound.

NICK MORAN

While Guy was in the post-production suite working on putting the film together, Matthew Vaughn was trying to get this film sold. This was a major task. After all, it had a first-time director, no star names, a footballer turned actor and cast of real gangsters. Not an easy sell. He took this film out there and touted it around to all the distributors without much response. Just when it looked like *Lock, Stock and Two Smoking Barrels* wasn't going to get picked up and might never see the light of day, he got an offer from Polygram films. He didn't like the offer and so he shopped around but still got no response: 'There's nobody in this film. No one's ever heard of these guys.' Matthew went back to Polygram and managed to work out a deal that everyone was happy with. One of the things that came out of Polygram coming on board was that Guy got to go through their whole back catalogue of music, from which he created one of the best soundtrack albums ever.

> That album went platinum; everybody had a copy. I couldn't walk into a pub for two years without a song from it being played. For the first year I never twigged, and I thought it was a right coincidence that it would be playing at the same time as I was in there. Then I started to notice the little looks as I came in and the barman would disappear out back and then James Brown would come on, or 'Liar Liar'.

NICK MORAN

Matthew is a brilliant producer who has a earned himself a lot of love and respect.

> Matthew wanted to be in the film business, and managed, through his family, to get a job in Los Angeles after leaving Stowe School. He was working for the William Morris agency as an agent's assistant. He was basically standing by the copy machine copying contracts etc. and listening to actors' agents on the phones doing deals with the studios. Then he came back to London and he decided that he wanted to be a producer so he was actively asking people in the business that he knew if they knew anyone who had written a script and to get them to send it to him. So he was reading lots of scripts when *Lock, Stock* dropped on his desk. It was a page turner.
> Matthew got in touch with Guy. Guy had been getting lots of offers to buy the script, but for other people to direct. He didn't

want that, he wanted to direct it himself. Matthew was the first person to come along who understood what Guy wanted, and he was the only one willing to let him do that and to not try to get the script off him. That's why they hit it off.

Matthew then approached all the usual film industry finance houses with this director who'd only done a short and who had this script in which he proposed to use real gangsters in some of the roles, about some kids growing weed. No one wanted to touch it. Those finance houses wouldn't even return Matthew's calls. So he decided to go to other people that he'd met in other parts of his life. Stowe School was one of the country's premier public schools, so he had a lot of contacts who were in a good financial situation. Trudie Styler came on board and so did Stephen Marks, and then others followed.

SIMON HAYES

Don't underestimate Matthew. He may look like a public school boy, but he's smarter than most people.

TIM MAURICE-JONES

Matthew Vaughn pulled it all together; he was great as producer. I said to him once, 'You should consider directing because you really get on so well with actors.' Now look at him. He did get on with all the actors – not that producers don't often get on with actors, but Matt really did. Good man, Matthew Vaughn. Good, good man. He worked harder than anybody to get this film to completion and out there, because he loved it and believed in it.

VAS BLACKWOOD

The hands-on thing that Matt did as a producer was amazing, I mean, so diligent, and that's quite aside from all the bullshit that he did to get the thing made in the first place. As a producer Matt did all of the things you take for granted. Matt made sure the marketing was right; Matt got Freud's (PR company) involved. He oversaw every aspect of the distribution.

NICK MORAN

Matt also did the one thing that changed the film completely and that I think made it the hit it was. He organised a test screening.

The film was shown to a mixed audience and they gave their critique of the film. The general consensus was that it was brilliant except for one thing. There was originally a storyline involving a woman who was the girlfriend of Eddie, the sister of Winston. Nearly all of the comments that came back from the screening were that they didn't really understand why this character was in the film. It was decided to cut that character out, and this made the film a complete lads' caper movie.

Cutting this storyline out left a huge gap in the film, however, and that meant that lots of reshoots were needed. Guy's genius comes to the fore again, as he had only one night to rewrite and one day to do the reshoots. A lot was changed. You can generally tell what it is by the fact that Jason Flemyng is wearing a beanie hat in the reshoot scenes, as they were shot nearly nine months after the wrap and he had gone onto another job and grown his hair, which he couldn't cut. The ending was originally Nick and the girl driving off in the AC Cobra, followed by Vinnie and Little Chris in a battered old car, leaving it very open for a sequel.

Guy literally wrote the new ending overnight on the back of a fag packet, this is before emails, and he read it down the phone to me: 'you say "get rid of them guns", and then Vinnie comes in, and then you say … and he says … and you say …'

He read it out and I said, 'It sounds great, super.'

'So that's what we're doing tomorrow.' It was literally like that; that was the way he made it up. There were lots of good pick-ups shot, including 'guns for show, knives for a pro', the getting drunk scene with Statham doing his back flips and setting light to a £20 quid note like a cigar, the scene with Sting in the car, The big scene with Vinnie and us trying to phone Flemyng …

NICK MORAN

A big problem for the reshoots was funding: they didn't have any, and Matthew had exhausted all his friends with money. So Jason Flemyng stepped in to help.

'I'd just done a film called *Deep Rising* and had some money. We needed to do some reshoots and Matt said to me, 'Would you put some money in?' He needed fifty grand so I gave him fifty grand. He said, 'Look, you'll be last in but first out, and I'll give you half a per cent.' So I was ok. He was a man of his word.

JASON FLEMYNG

'can we lock up and get drunk now?'

Ed, Tom amd Bacon discuss the card game.

The boys celebrate a job well done.

Lock, Stock and Two Smoking Barrels premiered at the Haymarket Cinema on 25 August 1998. It was released in cinemas three days later. For a cast of new boys who had never been in anything like this before it was wonderful madness. The crowds were lined up on the street, the press were lined up along the red carpet and the place was full of celebrities, including Dustin Hoffman, Anna Friel and Ewan McGregor. You know, there is nothing more ego boosting than going down a red carpet and having the entire place there to see you. I've been lucky enough to be on a few red carpets, and stupid enough to miss one too … more on that later.

A bunch of us rented a limo for the night – me, Frank Harper, Steve Sweeney, Huggy Leaver, Tony McMahon and Ronnie Fox. I met them at Charing Cross station. They were already half-cut on champagne, having started from somewhere in South London, so I was met with cheers, shouts and lots of buzz. We drove round to the Haymarket Cinema. We got there a little early, so we made the driver take a slow drive by the drop-off point so we could check out who else was early. As he slowly moved through the fenced-off lane of traffic leading to the drop-off point there were fans craning to see through the tinted windows – I guess they were hoping for it to be Madonna. They were going to be sorely disappointed. When we came around the second time and stopped, the fans all got very excited and began to cheer. The press started pulling their cameras up, ready to snap the latest celeb to arrive. When this bunch of lads who nobody recognised got out of the car, they literally froze. The cameras went away and the cheering stopped instantly. At this stage nobody knew that we were all in the film. We went inside the foyer and there was a huge buzz of excitement – lots of noise and people talking very loudly. Flemyng, Statham, Moran and Fletcher were in front of the poster with their faces on it, being mobbed by the press for interviews and pictures. Actually, when I say Nick Moran was being interviewed that's not strictly true, because at this point he was being hidden in a broom cupboard so that he wasn't nicked by the police.

I went to the premiere with me mum and dad. We got out of the car and they went inside while I did some photos. I'm standing there and Dustin Hoffman tries to sneak in behind me and the photographers are going mental to get a picture of him. There's this fella going, 'Get out of the way, pal, I want a picture of Dustin.' I said to him, 'I'm the star of this fuckin' film.' He goes 'I don't care who you fuckin' are, get out the way, you cunt.' And he tries to move me by pulling my tie and it rips. Well, that was it. The blood just rose up. I hit him as hard as I could and he collapsed on the floor, and then everyone took a picture of him. I got whisked away, and I told Guy that I'd just punched a photographer. The police got called and Guy hid me in a broom cupboard. Guy was like, 'You're not going anywhere,' and he hid in this broom cupboard until the police had gone. It was only later, at the after event, that it hit me. 'Oh my God, what have I done, what have I done?' Then the next day the press ran all this stuff. The geezer was pressing charges, so Matt sorted me out with a decent solicitor who tells me I can't go with self-defence because I could have pulled away. He's charged me with wounding and got all these statements and shit. So I went in to the police, and while everyone else is doing *TFI Friday*, I'm locked up. Because I'm with a good brief, I walk back out. Mad thing is, they get this statement from one of the security guards which was just, 'He called him a cunt so Nick stuck one on him.' If you read the statement it just keeps saying, 'He called him a cunt so he stuck one on him.' So I had a proper trial at the Old Bailey. They kept it quiet. Statham came down with me.

We're all sat in there, and the prosecution is like, 'It was a hot day, and my client's livelihood relies on pictures of celebrities, and he'd been in the press pit for two hours waiting for people to arrive. The accused walked in and obscured the view of a celebrity. My client playfully pushed him and used a jocular rude word …'

And the judge says, 'What rude word was this?'

'I beg your pardon your honour?'

'What was the rude word?'

'Um … the word was … "cunt", your honour.'

'He called him a cunt?'

'Yes, your honour. A cunt, your honour.'

It was like the best Peter Cook and Dudley Moore sketch. Statham is pissing himself and is snorting into his hands. It was fucking brilliant. Then they took me off into chambers and my brief says the judge will reduce it to affray, which is the lowest you can have, if I plead guilty. And that'll be the end of it. I couldn't really say I didn't do it, so I pleaded guilty to affray and got a fine of about sixty quid.

NICK MORAN

There's another story from the premiere involving Dustin Hoffman:

We met at the Dorchester – all the boys, Vinnie, Trudie, Sting, Guy and Matthew, a few others, and Dustin Hoffman. We were all having some champagne, and Dustin Hoffman is standing talking to me and he says, 'You are brilliant, you are so good in this film.'

'Really? Thank you, Dustin. You seen the film then?'

'No.'

I was pissing myself all night.

VAS BLACKWOOD

On the red carpet at the London premiere at The Haymarket. From left to right: Ann Byrne, Dustin Hoffman, Sting, Trudie Styler.

For me the premiere was the first time I saw the film, but a lot of the cast had seen the film at various screenings already.

I went to a screening in one of those little screening rooms in Soho. At the time I was doing a TV thing called *Boys Unlimited*. I went with two of the producers. I said, 'Do you want to come and see this film I shot last year,' and again I was a bit dazed by it all. They're kind of like, 'That's fucking brilliant, that's fucking brilliant. That's going to be fucking massive.'

FRANK HARPER

Ewan McGregor.

Vinnie Jones.

Noel Gallagher arrives at the after party.

Anna Friel has some fun outside the after party. Ronnie Fox can be seen peeking his head in.

I'd seen it before at a screening in the west end. It was an early morning thing. Sid Owen turned up, I don't know how, but he was there with his brothers. I said to Guy after, 'Vinnie's really good.' Vinnie was my favourite character; his role is really good. I said to Guy, 'That Vinnie's good.' He said, 'You're not too bad yourself.' So I'd seen it, and I knew it was a bit special.

VAS BLACKWOOD

I remember sitting in my seat and waiting nervously. I had no idea what the film was going to be like. When we read the script we knew it had potential, and when we were shooting it we knew that Guy knew what he was doing and the cast were fantastic, but the script and the shoot are only part of the film-making process. A great film can be ruined in the edit or made in the edit, and I was nervous about which this one was going to be.

Once I'd seen it, I was blown away. I loved the look, with the sepia tones, and the soundtrack, a great use of the music. The acting was brilliant by everybody. Not one person stood out for being bad, from the leads down to the cameos. The comic timing was spot on. I came out thinking, 'This film is great and it's going to be a huge hit, and I'm lucky enough to be in it!' Of course nobody knew how much of a hit it was going to be. You can never tell that until it gets out there.

I remember being taken aback by the sheer scale of it. I went away on holiday with the family and we got a cab into town and passed a massive billboard, and that was just like, 'Oh my God, look.' That was the first time I got a sense of 'they're going to town on this'. Also, it had been quite quick in post-production, because normally you can wait a long time before a film comes out. Eight months felt incredibly quick for it to be launched like that. I remember being swept along by the scale of it. The distributors [Polygram] were getting right behind it.

There was a big introduction on stage at the beginning with the boys. When the film came on I was sat behind Keith Allen and he was just roaring with laughter and having a great time and really enjoying the humour of it.

At the end I was ushered into a stretch limo and taken to the party. We went to a club in Mayfair. The limo was rammed with people, lots of actors that I knew from other films, all being really buzzy about the film – 'Oh God, it's amazing, you're amazing' – there was just this electric wild atmosphere in this limo, and after that I don't really remember much else about the evening.

STEVEN MACKINTOSH

Nobody seems to remember the after party, including me. I don't think it means it was a dull party – in fact, I suspect it may mean the exact opposite. Nick Rowe, who played J, must have had a particularly good time – he can't even remember the premiere!

I went to some screening and there was a lot of us there … Do you know what? I don't remember if that was the premiere. Where did we go after?

NICHOLAS ROWE

The red carpet premiere I missed was for a film called *Quills*. I did the film in 1999, just after *Lock, Stock* came out. It starred Kate Winslet, Joaquin Pheonix, Michael Caine and the fantastic Geoffrey Rush. It was about the Marquis de Sade and his incarceration in Charenton lunatic asylum in France. I was Bouchon, an executioner who had gone mad from cutting off so many heads during the French Revolution. Bouchon kills Kate Winslet, which was fun (in a nice way). I got on really well with the producer, Peter Kaufman, and the director, Phillip Kaufman, and we joked about me flying out to LA for the premiere. So I did. Peter told me that they had arranged a ticket for me and the premiere was going to be on Wednesday, so I flew out on the Sunday so I could recover from the jet lag. I stayed with my friends out in Woodland Hills, close to the Kardashians' place (I didn't see them). On Monday morning I contacted the office and they faxed over my tickets. I didn't even look at them. I just put them on the side and settled into the day.

The next day Phillip Kaufman called up: 'Where were you?'

'When?'

'Last night. At the theatre. There were two empty seats where you and your guest were supposed to be sitting. I was going to introduce you to the whole of Hollywood.'

I was dumbstruck. I couldn't speak and I felt sick. I had just blown my big chance of breaking it in Hollywood and all because I thought the premiere was on Wednesday, not Monday, and I didn't read the ticket.

Lock, Stock and Two Smoking Barrels is the one thing I get recognised for most, and I think that applies to everyone who was in it – except maybe Vinnie Jones, who obviously gets recognised for being Vinnie Jones, and nowadays Jason Statham may get recognised for being in just about every action movie out there. I bet he never thought, when he was selling dodgy gear out of a suitcase in Oxford Street, that he'd end up a huge movie star.

Not long after the film came out, I was on a train coming into Charing Cross. As the train clattered its way slowly over Hungerford Bridge coming into Charing Cross Station, I prepared to get off and was waiting by the sliding doors. I was aware of somebody looking at me. I kept looking ahead, not wanting to make eye contact – after all, I'm a Londoner and Londoners don't make contact for fear of actually having to interact with each other. Just as the train was coming to a halt, this young fella standing next to me said, 'Are you an actor?'

Now, to this day, I never know how to reply to that question, which I get a lot. I can either reply with 'Yes, of course I am. You may recognise me from such films as ...' and sound like Troy McClure from *The Simpsons*, or just smile and say 'yes'. I generally tend to just smile and feel very self-conscious, which is what I did on this day.

He continued, 'Are you in *Lock, Stock and Two Smoking Barrels*?'

'Yes.'

'I thought so. You was Nick The Greek, right?'

'Yes.'

'Fuckin' excellent, mate. You're a legend.'

He turned and shouted across the carriage to his mates: 'You'll never guess who this is. It's that Nick The Greek from *Lock, Stock and Two Smoking Barrels*.'

With that recognition by one not so quiet person, I was suddenly being stared at by the whole carriage, and when the doors opened, walking along the platform I was inundated by people wanting my autograph. I felt like a pop star. Not a very good pop star, 'cause I can't sing, but a pop star. This was the only occasion when I was actually mobbed, but to this day every time *Lock, Stock* is on the television, the next day I get recognised two or three times, and even if it hasn't been on for a while I still get recognised probably once or twice a week.

Getting recognised on a train is probably one of the nicest ways for it to happen. The worst experiences I've had – and it's been more than once – have been when I'm in a club or pub toilet. I'll be standing there having a pee. Somebody will come up and stand next to me, and I'll feel their eyes burning into me. They're often drunk – not staggering drunk, but drunk enough to have the courage to say something to me in a public toilet while I've got my willy out. The conversation will always go something like:

'Are you that actor?'

'Which actor is that then?'

'That Greek fella in that film?'

Once we have established that I am that Greek fella called Nick in *Lock, Stock*, they nearly always ask for an autograph, or to shake my hand.

My reply is always, 'My hand is a little busy at the moment. Can I see you outside?'

Outside in the bar they will have told their mates, and I'll get a cheer, then I'll sign some autographs and do some selfies.

The biggest cheer I ever had was when I went with my mate Jonathan Moore to the Shed Bar in Stamford Bridge. Johnny is another actor/director who I've known since I started in this business. We worked together on my first movie, *My Beautiful Laundrette*, directed by Stephen Frears and starring Daniel Day-Lewis, a controversial film about an interracial gay relationship. Johnny and I also did a play called *Arrivederci Millwall*, about footy hooligans going to Spain for the 1982 World Cup to avenge a comrade who

My Beautiful Laundrette. From left to right: Richard Graham, Johnny Moore, Daniel Day-Lewis, me, Dawn Archibald.

was killed in the Falklands War. I learned that Johnny was a Chelsea fan, and he invited me to go with him to watch Chelsea play live on TV in the shed bar at Stamford Bridge stadium. At half time I went to the loo and was recognised, and when I came out I was greeted by the entire bar chanting, 'We've got Nick The Greek, we've got Nick The Greek, we got, we got, we got, we got, we got Nick The Greek.' Now that was funny. Recently I was told that the story has grown somewhat – to such an extent that when I came back from the toilet the entire crowd of 41,000 people were chanting!

All the cast have some kind of recognition story.

I was in south London and I saw a black Audi go round this corner really fast and knock this bloke off his bike and drive off. This guy went straight onto his arse and cut up all his elbows and knees. I was like, 'those idiots', so I put my foot down and I followed them down to the Wandsworth one-way system. I pulled in front of the car. I was furious. I got out of the car and I went, 'Mate, you just knocked someone off their bike.' The doors of the car opened and these three huge gangsters got out. And I mean huge, to the point where my knees buckled and I had to hold onto my car. I thought, 'Oh my God, I'm gonna die.' They were furious. They were like, 'What is wrong with you?' And then one of them says, 'Bruv, it's Fat Tom,' and they were all like, 'Oh, hello mate.' I thought, 'Oh my God,' I was so relieved. My life has been saved two or three times by being Fat Tom.

There was another time when I was outside Hamleys and these two people came up and wanted a picture. So I put my arm round the girl. I was a bit grumpy because I was trying to get presents for my brother's kids, and I put my arm round the girl and I said

'Go on then, be quick,' and she was like, 'No, can you take a picture of us?'

It happens every day, particularly on planes. I always hope that it's going to be for one of my other films, like the one about the lesbian sheep farmer that I loved, but no, it's always bloody *Lock, Stock*.

JASON FLEMYNG

As soon as the film was out I was getting recognised. I used to get it anyway, from *The Lenny Henry Show* and *Only Fools and Horses*. Right up until a couple of days ago. I get people pull out the camera and they want me to say the lines, and, you know what, I do it for them. That's how I roll. It's a part of me; I don't turn my nose up at it.

VAS BLACKWOOD

I don't get recognised from it until I speak. It's because of the hair, because of the wig. So it's not given me recognition, but what it has given me is kudos with a certain age group once they found out I was in it. It's very cool to have been in it, that's the key thing. It's very cool, more so than anything else I've ever done.

VICTOR MCGUIRE

The *Lock, Stock* thing didn't work for me. I went to a testimonial/celebrity football match at Old Trafford. Robbie Williams was playing and my mate, who was playing for England at the time. Terry Venables loved my mate and had him on for the whole game. It was quite a good game and I was in the bar after and I was thinking, 'There's all these great footballers, Peter Schmeichel, there's Edgar

Davids, there's Steve McManaman and Jamie Redknapp.' I couldn't get served, even though people were looking at me and thinking they knew me from somewhere. It didn't work, because we come absolutely second to all these great football players, quite rightly. Sometimes it works the other way round, but not this time. I couldn't get served even when it had calmed down, and Jamie Redknapp had to buy me a drink. I offered to pay for it, but he said no. He produced this enormous wad of cash, like your character [Nick The Greek] in the film. I didn't realise footballers carried around big wads of cash. I just thought they just nodded and got a drink.

NICHOLAS ROWE

When the film first came out in the cinemas the whole cast was the toast of the town. Sadly, I was out of town on tour with the National Theatre. The play was *Cleo, Camping, Emmanuelle and Dick*, a brilliant play set behind the scenes on some of the *Carry On* films and mainly focused on the relationship between Sid James and Barbara Windsor. I played a fictitious character who was kind of based on Ronnie Knight, Barbara Windsor's husband for twenty-one years and an East London gangster. We toured all over the country for about six months – all of which was during the release period of *Lock, Stock*, so I missed out on nearly all of the jollies that went on. I was able to get back for the premiere and for the *Empire* Magazine Awards. The awards dinner was a daytime thing and it was mad. A lot of the cast was there to see Guy receive the award for Best British Film from Joan Collins. We had a table that was the noisiest table there and that consumed a lot of alcohol. Everybody did manage to behave during the awards ceremony but afterwards it got rowdy, or so I was told.

I had to leave to get back to North Wales for the show that night. As I was leaving I saw Steve Sweeney (Plank) trying to get friendly with Julie Hesmondhalgh – you would recognise her as Hayley from *Coronation Street*. As I said, I had to leave before it got too messy, so I didn't actually see whether his not too subtle advances were accepted or rejected.

There was one night out in Soho that ended up at a club that was very trendy at the time, Titanic in Brewer Street. It was the sister club to the Atlantic Bar in Air Street, round the corner. Me and my mates were walking towards the club and I accidentally caught the eye of one of the door staff; I wasn't trying to. He saw me and turned to one of his buddies, they had a little conversation, and as we got to the long line waiting to go in, he parted the crowd and gestured me through into the club and on into the VIP area, where we sat and were waited on hand and foot. I've never had anything so cool happen in my life ever again, it was like being a Hollywood star or something. I mean, how cool is it to walk towards a club and have the crowd parted and just to walk in without stopping?

I think that was probably the moment I truly realised what a huge thing this film was going to be and how much difference it was going to make to a lot of people's lives.

Not long after the film came out I was in Nottingham shooting *A Room for Romeo Brass*, and all the cast said, 'Oh we're going to go and see a film Friday after we finish work. Do you wanna come?' I went, 'Yeah, yeah.' But they've booked tickets for *Lock, Stock*, so I'm now sitting in this cinema trying to hide. I thought, 'If anyone sees me, they're gonna think, "Look at that prat, sitting in the cinema watching his own film."' And people were roaring with laughter and I'm thinking, 'Fuck yeah, this is a hit film.' The cinema's full and everyone is really enjoying it. Once the film come out all of us couldn't walk down the street anymore.

FRANK HARPER

I got invited to the Elle Style Awards, and I thought there'd been a mistake but I'd go anyway. Ray Winstone had been invited. Me and Ray had the same agent, and the agent invited himself: 'Come to the office and we'll go to this thing together.' I had a suit I'd borrowed. It was the first time I'd been to a thing where the paparazzi were there and lots of cool people were there and the paparazzi were making a fuss over me, and I realised, 'I'm not an interloper. I'm not a blagger.' That was probably the first moment I twigged that it was all alright.

NICK MORAN

I knew it was going to be a success the moment I read the script. I knew that if we got this right it was going to be so good. I knew when I saw it with an audience, from the reaction, that it was going to be so good. I was sat in the cinema with people and the reaction was through the roof. I'd never seen anything like this before.

TIM MAURICE-JONES

'it's a samoan pub'

Samoan Joe.

Bacon, Soap and Tom go for a nice refreshing drink.

The craziness carried on for quite a while, with all sorts of opening premieres and shoots. As I've said earlier, I was on tour in *Cleo, Camping, Emmanuelle and Dick* for the National Theatre when the film opened, so I missed out on nearly all the award ceremonies, the shoots and the blagging sessions. But I did do a couple of them. One was a promo for Film4 when they were showing a collection of crime movies over the Easter weekend. They got some of us together to play a card game and introduce the films, which included *Daylight Robbery* with Ewan McGregor, and Quentin Tarantino's *Reservoir Dogs*. There was me, Nick Moran, Jason Statham, Jason Flemyng, Dexter Fletcher and Vas Blackwood, and the main thing I remember was Vas totally winding Nick Moran up. I forget what was actually said, but Vas got Nick so wound that it nearly came to blows. It may have been about Nick's card playing skills.

The Film4 promo shoot.

From, left to right:
Vinnie Jones, Dale
Winton, Davina McCall,
me.

*Above: Chris Coleman
with Suzi Perry. Right:
Actor Stephen Marcus*

OK!

IRST FOR CELEBRITY NEWS

EXCLUSIVE PARTY COVERAGE

**MODELS 1
CELEBRATES ITS
30TH BIRTHDAY**

THE STARS CELEBRATE AT HARVEY NICKS

RADCLIFFE REVELRY

JORDAN BOOSTS MARK'S NEW PLACE

Jordan, Dean Gaffney and TV presenter Suzi Perry were among the guests at the opening of Mark Fuller's latest venture, The Radcliffe in Hampshire. Other stars at the restaurant and bar launch included *Big Brother* lovers Alex Sibley and Melanie Hill, and *Lock, Stock And Two Smoking Barrels* star Stephen Marcus. The Radcliffe is a joint venture between Mark, Garry Hollihead, Lorri Seymour and Nigel Nieddu.

*Above: Dean Gaffney, Sammi Jayne and Jerri
Byrne. Top middle: Mark Fuller with Garry and
... Top left: Sammi with Jordan.*

*Clockwise from left: Model Lisa Butcher; socialite Miss Dee
Kicking presenters Ortis and Sarah Cawood; British b...
Lennox Lewis; and singer, DJ and outrageous fashion icon*

10 COVENT GARDEN

OFFICIAL OPENING FOR GLITTERING VENUE

Following the success of City Bars & Restaurants' 10 Room in Piccadilly Circus and 10 Tokyo Joe's in Mayfair, 10 Covent Garden was launched with a star-studded party. The 900-capacity club – designed by Keith Hobbs and Linzi Copple – saw one of the largest parties of the year so far and celebrity guests included Lisa Butcher, Boy George and Macaulay Culkin.

*Below, from left: Stephen Marcus and Nick Bateman; Alex
Marques and Ivo Costa; Madame Melville stars Macaulay Culkin
and Irène Jacob; and Jack White and Marie-Helene Cockow*

The opening of
The Radcliff, a
club in Fareham,
Hampshire.

The opening of 10
Covent Garden. I'm
with 'Nasty Nick'
from the first series
of *Big Brother*. Nick
Moran was also
at this do – at the
time he and I would
happily go to the
opening of a fridge!

119

A while after that I got a call from my new agent. *Loaded* magazine wanted to do a shoot with most of the cast. The shoot was at Holborn Studios on Shepherdess Walk, by Regents Canal. It's used for fashion and pop promos mainly, with the occasional small movie shoot. It's been used by iconic photographers like Annie Leibovitz, David Bailey, Terry O'Neill (who was once married to Vera Day, who plays the croupier in the card game, which as you know is the centre of the whole *Lock, Stock* story). There's a long list of movie stars who have shot there, including Ray Winstone, Kate Blanchett, Emma Thompson, Hugh Grant, Pierce Brosnan, I could go on forever. They've had iconic bands (Black Sabbath, The Clash), they've had casts from shows and films, and, of course us, the cast of *Lock, Stock and Two Smoking Barrels*.

The shoot itself was of all of us in the various groups mucking about in designer suits. Nothing more than that, but it was a nice piece for *Loaded*, as you can see from the photographs. Unfortunately I'm a big fella, and no designer makes suits for the fuller-figured man, so I had to provide my own – which wasn't a problem. When it was accessorised properly with a fedora, I looked some big old jazz musician. As far as I recall, the shoot went off without a hitch and a good laugh was had by all, except at the end of the day when some suits went missing. I don't know if they were found or not.

Talking of suits, the four boys got to go to a lot of product events – film stars and celebrities are invited to a store to basically pick whatever they would like from the latest lines. In return the store or designers gets famous people wearing their gear, and it all helps to create the dream life that the general public will pay for.

LOCK
STOCK
THE
F*****
LOT
YOU
HAVE
BEEN
WATCHING. . .

(from top left to right)
Guy Ritchie
(writer/director), Jason
'Tom' Flemyng, Nick
'Eddy' Moran, Jason
'Bacon' Statham, Dexter
'Soap' Fletcher, Jake
'Dean' Abraham, Victor
'Gary' McGuire, Frank
'Dog' Harper, Steve
'Plank' Sweeney, Huggy
'Paul' Lever, Ronnie
'Mickey' Fox

Vas 'Rory Breaker'
Blackwood, Stephen
'Nick The Greek'
Marcus, Tony 'John'
McMahon, Robert
'traffic warden' Brydon,
Steve 'Winston'
Mackintosh, Nicholas 'J'
Rowe, Nick 'Charles'
Marcq, Charlie 'William'
Forbes

The *Loaded* photo shoot.

(Bottom left)
Suit model's own.
Charcoal zip-front jacket
£100 and trousers £60 by
JOHN by Johns Richmond
for Debenhams

(Opposite page, left to right) Navy three-quarter length coat £475 by Aquascutum and house check shirt starting from £80 by Burberry Brown pinstripe suit, jacket £379 and trousers £149 by Christophe Lemaire and crush tonic shirt £50 by Yves Saint Laurent Pour Homme

Grey single-breasted suit £750 by Ken Odiniah White shirt £90 by Oswald Boateng black loafers £175 by Nicole Farhi

Combie coat Oswald Boateng suit and white shirt, tie and loafers all by Gucci — model's own White single-breasted suit £350 by Issac white, red and blue knitted jersey £118 by Byblos and white loafers £250 by Thierry Mugler

(This page, left to right) White single breasted suit £495 by CK Calvin Klein and black shirt £285 by Prada Fawn three-quarter length coat £425 and navy all-in-one suit from a selection both by Copperwheat Blundell tan hat £36 by Kangol

(Small pic, right, left to right) Grey mohair suit £350 by Marks & Spencer grey vest £34.99 by River Island and black leather sandals £80 by Hudson Navy pinstripe suit £725 and purple shirt £140 both by Richard James black side-zip ankle boots £54.99 by Next Blue frock coat £400 by Copperwheat Blundell slate grey shirt £18.95 by River Island window-pane check trousers (part of suit) £445 by Richard James brogue slingbacks £260 by Jeffery West for Copperwheat Blundell

LOCK
STOCK
THE
F*****
LOT

(left to right)
Navy shirt £74 and navy tie
£30 both by **Emporio
Armani**, black belt £10 by
Marks & Spencer, black
three-quarter length mac
£475 by **Burberry**
Green single breasted suit
£380 by **Idol mui**, white
short-sleeve jersey £61 by
John Smedley and cream
suede loafers £150 by
Giorgio Armani
Suit, shirt and tie model's
own, Blanford trilby £32 by
Kangol, purple check suit
£895 and stripe shirt £130
both by **Oswald Boateng**

Black single breasted suit;
jacket £399 and trousers
£199 by **Nicole Farhi** and
cream short-sleeve shirt
£49.99 by **Morgan
Homme**
Green double-breasted coat
from a selection and sky
blue safari suit; jacket £505
and trousers £180 all by
**Vivienne Westwood
Man Collection**
heathered cloth relaxed
draw-string pant suit £275
by **Massimo Osti** sky blue
jersey £61 by **John
Smedley**

Me, Nick, Dex and Stath, we were, like, the four boys, so we got most of the attention. We got this thing – I think Nick started it – where we would see how many suits we could blag. I think Nick got up to nineteen. We were in Gucci with them saying, 'Have whatever suits you want. Basically we were all skint: Nick was living in a squat in an old pub, Statham was driving around in a white transit van – dating Kelly Brook and picking her up in a transit van. Dexter was about to go to America, but was homeless at the time. So the fact we could blag nineteen suits from New Bond Street was exciting. Nick sold those suits on.

JASON FLEMYNG

(Above) left to right as before *Lock, Stock And Two Smoking Barrels* is out to rent on video on 1 March. We've got 10 copies of the video and soundtrack to give away. See News pages for details.

LOCK STOCK THE F***** LOT

(this page, left to right)
Navy three-piece suit £165 by **Yves Saint Laurent**; blue-grey shirt £81 by **John Smedley** and navy silk tie £50.05 by **Crombie**.
Cream single-breasted suit £165 and lilac shirt £81 both by **Thierry Mugler**.

(Breakpic right) Navy pinstripe single-breasted suit £285.95 by **WoodHouse** plus striped tie £49 by **Oswald Boateng** black loafers £79.99 by **Barratts**

(far right) Black leather jacket £650 by **Raffle** and navy pinstripe suit £195 by **Oswald Boateng**; blue-finish shirt £49.99 by **Copenhagen Menswear** and navy silk tie £50 by **River Island**. (far right) **Richard James** Grey check suit £485, cream shirt from £110 and black tie £39 all by **Mulberry**. (above) suit to right coat £285 by **Austin Reed**; blue shirt £50 by **Gieves & Hawkes**.

LOCK
STOCK
THE
F*****
LOT

LOCK
STOCK
THE
F*****
LOT

They're tryin' to fit us up! Classy suits worn by the Smoking Barrels boys

story: BETH SUMMERS photos: DANIEL SMITH

Left?
Dark grey single-breasted
suit £995 by **Giorgio
Armani**, blue cotton shirt
£65 and floral tie £50 both
by **Jasper Conran** black,
single-breasted suit £298
and black shirt £65 both by
Agnes B grey tie £14.99
by **River Island**

This page, left to right
hooded navy blouson
£279, matching trousers
£169 and white cropped
shirt £129 all by **Emporio
Armani**
Cream leather coat £1,057
to order by **Ruffo** navy
blue suit £395 by **Bailey**
blue cotton shirt £24.99 by
Next
Floral applique three-piece
suit: jacket £825, trousers

£225 and waistcoat £305
all by **Paul Smith**
white cotton shirt £83 by
Agnes B

Gucci gave us suits and it became a competition to see who could get the most suits. I ended up with nearly forty. We got taken to a product placement company. It was on the King's Road: 'Come to our boutique and have some sunglasses.'

Dexter was a bit of an old hand at these. We get in the taxi afterwards and he's got loads. I'm like, 'Ooh I'll have a pair of D&Gs.'

They're like, 'Take two.'

'Thank you. What do I have to do?'

'Just wear them.'

Then it became this thing where people gave us stuff.

NICK MORAN

Nobody gave me anything. I know, poor me. But I did get a decent career out of it, and lots of fun and memories, so I'm not complaining.

When the film got released, Matthew Vaughn went above and beyond the job of a producer. He kept his finger on that film and drove it forward. He kept on top of all the marketing, to the point of going round the cinemas, checking they were doing what they should be. Most producers sit back and let the distribution company do it. If Matt found something wrong about it, he would be straight on the phone to Polygram and make sure they fixed it.

When it came out on release me and Matt got in his VW Golf and drove around every cinema we could making sure all the posters were right and I would get in the queue pretending to buy some tickets. I got into a massive argument with some bloke because he wanted to see *Rush Hour*. I went, 'You don't wanna see that, you wanna see *Lock, Stock and Two Smoking Barrels*.'

'Why would I wanna see that, that's shit.'

'You what?'

'It's fucking shit.'

'It's what?'

'It's fucking shit.'

'You fucking what?'

Matt pulled me away. Me and Matt bought tickets on the first Thursday afternoon at all the key sites. The hands-on thing that Matt did as a producer was amazing.

Also, the boys would go out to screenings together. They'd make a night of it and cruise the cinemas in the West End.

NICK MORAN

We used to meet on a Friday night, get a few drinks down us and then go to all the cinemas around Leicester Square and stand at the back and watch the audiences pissing themselves. Vinnie, Guy, Nick, Flemyng, Jason Statham, and Matthew if he was about. It was packed, and they'd be laughing, and we'd start laughing. We'd come out and go to another one, it was in about eight cinemas down there. It was in every cinema down there, and if we couldn't get in that one we'd go to another one. We'd say, 'What ya doin' tomorrow?' and we'd start at the Punch Bowl in Mayfair. Guy ended up buying that pub because of that.

VAS BLACKWOOD

In February 1999, six months after the UK premiere, the film opened in America. Although it had been a huge success in England, getting a deal in America wasn't as easy as you might think. Once again the lack of 'star' names that the American audiences would know was an issue. Nor did it have a star director or producer. In America it truly is a business, and

Poster on Sunset Strip, Los Angeles.

if the numbers aren't going to add up or the names aren't involved then it's more than likely a no go. I've heard stories about American television shows that have been piloted and picked up by the broadcaster, but the main cast member has been recast because the audience didn't like them or the execs didn't. A great example of that is *Star Trek*: in the pilot the captain was Christopher Pike, played by Jeffrey Hunter, but when it went to series it was James T. Kirk, played by William Shatner. So *Lock, Stock* was really up against it once more. Matthew had to do his magic producer work, and so he arranged some screenings for buyers in America, which were attended by a few noted celebrities.

The first person to see it and loved it was Madonna. Then she wanted to meet Guy. I remember Guy was like, 'Madonna wants to meet me. Will you all come along?' That was their first meeting and the rest is history.

Brad Pitt also saw it at a screening, but the one that swung it was Tom Cruise. Trudie Styler was a friend of Tom's, and they were struggling to get a buyer so she called up Tom and asked him if he'd come watch the film. He replied, 'Sure, send over a screener.' She said, 'No, would you go to a screening and watch it?' And he agreed. The room was full of potential buyers waiting for the film to start when Tom walked in and quietly took a seat in the front row. There was a buzz that went round the room. Tom loved the film, and laughed loud and hard all the way through the showing. At the end he walked out, thanking Matthew, and turned to all the buyers and just said, 'That film rocks.' Then all the buyers, to a man, got on their phones to the office, and within hours Matthew was in a the middle of a bidding war for a deal. The next day it was all over the Hollywood trade papers: 'Tom Cruise Says *Lock, Stock and Two Smoking Barrels* Rocks.' Tom Cruise really does have influence in Hollywood.

JASON FLEMYNG

The deal was done and now the tour would begin. Guy Ritchie, Jason Flemyng and Jason Statham toured nine cities, starting at the Sundance Film Festival in Aspen.

We became a little unit as it built up speed and ended up at Sundance, with Guy being courted by Robert Redford, and everybody loving the film.

NICK MORAN

Nick was at Sundance. Then we did a nine-city tour from Sundance to LA. We went to Washington and San Francisco and Boston and fuck knows where else. We flew together and stayed in big flash hotels and screened it in nine cities and it went really well. It went really, really well. We got to LA and they had a big premiere that they threw money at, with a party in a big old warehouse. That was on the Thursday and it came out on the Friday. We were meant to stay there for ten days. We were in the Four Seasons hotel and Vinnie Jones was doing singalongs with Liz Hurley and Samuel L. Jackson on the Saturday night. The box office figures came out on the Sunday morning and we were on the flight home by Sunday afternoon. They were like, 'Clear your room, you're leaving,' and I was like, 'No, no, no, we're here until Wednesday,' and because the numbers hadn't come up to what was expected they were like, 'No you're leaving.'

JASON FLEMYNG

They don't call it show *business* for nothing. *Lock, Stock* opened to $143,000 and grossed $3.7 million in America. Worldwide it grossed $28 million. Not bad for a film made for £800,000. Despite the poor showing at the box office, the film was still a huge success. It won loads of awards all over the world and got nominated for Best Picture several times; Guy won Best Director a few times too. But they didn't get the big ones.

Lock, Stock was up for BAFTAs. It didn't get one of them except the Audience Award, because they hate Guy and Matthew, the young upstarts. *Snatch* didn't even get nominated. They still don't get recognition. They hated us; we're not BAFTA material. You had all those 'Jewel of the Nile' type films being made and we came along and made *Lock, Stock* for less than their yearly salaries.

TIM MAURICE-JONES

I don't think they get the credit they deserve because they make commercial films.

FRANK HARPER

Here's a short selection of some of the awards it did get:

BAFTA – Audience Award
British Comedy Awards – Best Comedy Film
Empire Awards UK – Best British Film
Evening Standard British Film Awards – Most Promising
    Newcomer (Guy Ritchie)
MTV Movie Awards – Best New Film Maker
    (Guy Ritchie)
Tokyo International Film Festival – Best Director
    (Guy Ritchie)

At the BAFTAs. From left to right: Vinnie Jones, Jason Statham, Guy Ritchie, Matthew Vaughn, Nick Moran. Photo bombing: actor Martin Clunes.

Dexter, Guy, Jason and Jason on the red carpet at the Empire Magazine Awards.

Dexter gets surprised by P.H. Moriarty.

Steve Sweeney signing autographs.

One of the many reasons *Lock, Stock* was such a success was the style of it: the visual style, the comedic style, the camera style and the introduction of new ways of editing and shooting. When Guy was prepping for the shoot with Tim Maurice-Jones, he told Tim that he wanted him to be flash and show off with the camera. Tim is as responsible for the film's success as Guy or Matthew. Guy brilliantly chose Tim because of his body of work, and Tim took Guy's vision and made it exist.

I grew up loving *The Long Good Friday* and *Performance* and '60s gangster films. I was lighting it hard like an old movie sometimes. Sometimes it's modern and sometimes it's lit like something from the 1940s and '50s. It's dateless; the only thing that gives it away is the mobile phones. If you look at it, everything else could be today or the '60s. The idea was that we made it timeless. The clothes were kind of timeless; the art direction was timeless. We were very clear that we wanted it to have longevity. The great thing was that Guy had never directed a film … he'd done a short called *The Hard Case*. I wasn't a movie person. None of us were; we'd just done music videos, so we didn't know the rules. Our rules were just make it look cool. So most of the style is from music videos and stuff we were doing at the time. It wasn't to do with 'Is this the correct composition? Is this a complimentary close-up?' We did some scenes in just one shot, no close-up, no coverage, nothing. One shot on Steadicam. Like in Dog's office, when they've done the robbery and the boys are waiting, one or two takes on Steadicam, got it, move on. We did split screens, which are very '60s. We were showing off, being flash, not worrying about the rules. If they're somewhere and the light should be coming from the window, if it doesn't look good, don't do it. Make it look good. I think that's what gave it a real style.

I wanted to give it a look. I wanted to control the way it looked, impose my look on it.

TIM MAURICE-JONES

There was lots of talk about the visual, and how visually exciting it was going to be. Lots of talk about … lots of really interesting shots that the guys had been using on commercials and stuff that they were going to bring to the film.

There had never been a film quite like it, not of this style, except maybe those '60s gangster films like *Performance*, *Get Carter* or *Villain*. Tim was clearly influenced by the films he loved as a kid.

Some of the camera moves were fantastically innovative, and they also helped in its success because people were ready for a new way of telling the story. Guy and Tim and Peter Wignall, the camera operator, liked to use a lot of camera inside things. For example at the shop in the beginning the camera is inside the oven as Tom gets his money out and it's inside the pot of boiling carrots that Soap is cooking.

One of the most innovative camera moves was when Ed has lost in the card game and he's gone into shock, and the camera is part of his body. That rig has been used in so many films now. It was the first time I'd ever seen that kind of rig used in anything and it was so visually arresting. It's a great thing and it was so brilliantly done in that scene. He used the Stooges track 'I Wanna Be Your Dog'.

STEVEN MACKINTOSH

That shot was only supposed to be in the ring, but Nick was brilliant. He gets up, climbs through the ropes and walks towards the door. That's one of those happy accidents. I didn't expect that shot to go on that long. That rig didn't exist. We had to make it out of scaffold poles and we had to have someone holding the other end. It's been used in other films since, and that's a nice emulation.

TIM MAURICE-JONES

There were so many clever shots in there. They were planned. When I've got 8 stone of camera and scaffold poles strapped to me on a gurney and I'm walking out of a boxing ring, that's not, 'Oh, let's do this.'

NICK MORAN

That shot alone has been emulated by other film-makers. It's not stealing or copying or being unoriginal when another film-maker does what you did; it's paying homage to something you liked and admired. I did a film called *Sorted* in 2000, which used that camera rig idea. Matthew Rhys is in a club and his drink has been spiked and he's staggering around the club. Very obviously an homage.

It changed everything. There are so many wanna-be copies. I think it's wonderful, I love seeing films that copy us.

TIM MAURICE-JONES

Lock, Stock has produced a lot of similar films, and a lot of homages. Unfortunately very few if any have captured what it is that has made *Lock, Stock* so successful. They've mainly focused on aggression and violence, which is not in *Lock, Stock*, and they've missed the humour. And it's the humour that makes people love this film. That and the understanding of character.

I also think that every character in the film, somebody in the audience knows someone like that. I can't count the number of times I've been told that Nick The Greek reminds people of their mate who is also called Nick The Greek.

Guy's smart. Guy understands performance. Guy understands comedy, and he understands character. He had Vas, a black cockney, Stephen as a Greek without an accent, just the way people are in the east end. I think that's what gave it a grounding. Guy got a lot of stick for being a Mockney. The thing they don't get is Guy just loves the language, and when you mix with types of people you fall into their speech patterns. Guy was filming a London gangster film; he was having fun with the language.

There's a lot of love for this film, it's a British institution. There aren't many films that are beloved like that.

TIM MAURICE-JONES

lenny mcLean

Lenny McLean.

Lenny McLean was a much-loved actor. In *Lock, Stock* he played Barry The Baptist, so called because of his habit of drowning people for Hatchett Harry. During filming, Lenny had what he thought was a heavy cold. He went to a doctor, who at first diagnosed him with pleurisy. X-rays later showed that it was lung cancer. He died in Bexley in July 1998. Guy dedicated the film to him.

Lenny lived a colourful life, and probably made some bad decisions, but through it all he was a loving family man who adored his wife, Val, and his kids, Jamie and Kelly. Everybody who knew him liked and respected him. Well, maybe not everybody. But he did make an impact on everybody whose lives he touched. In this chapter I'm hopefully going to give you an inkling of that love and respect that he garnered from the cast and crew of *Lock, Stock*. I enjoyed a few conversations with him, and I definitely liked him and would have liked to have got to know him more.

Lenny McLean grew up without a dad, and he and his brothers were violently abused by his stepfather, Jim Irwin. The violence was stopped by their uncle, Jimmy Spinks, when he beat up Irwin and threatened to kill him if he ever hurt the kids again. Lenny spent a large part of his younger life on the other side of the law, getting arrested for various small crimes and running for local gangsters such as the Krays. He later became a good friend of Charlie Kray; they opened a pub called The Guv'nors. He discovered a skill at bare-knuckle fighting when he bought a car from local trader named Kenny Mac and it broke down within a couple of days. Lenny pushed the car on his own a couple of miles back to Kenny's to get his money back. Kenny Mac refused a refund, which was brave for a little fella, and said Lenny could earn his money back by fighting in a fight that Kenny had going on in his yard a few days later. Len fought a 7ft-tall, 20-stone opponent who lasted one minute. That was the start of his unlicensed bare-knuckle career. He had some monster fights and he was renowned for being a no-holds-barred fighter. He would often have to be separated from his beaten opponent by several men. This was because, Lenny said, he was fighting for the little vulnerable kid that he was when he was being beaten by Jim Irwin. He is famous for his rivalry with Roy Shaw. They hated each other and both claimed they were the best in the world. They fought three times. Brutally, Lenny lost the first and won the next two re-matches with first round knockouts. He was 'the king of bouncers' and had his own firm that ran most of the doors at club and raves in London throughout the 1980s and '90s. His favourite place was Camden Palace.

I've known Lenny for years from round the area, since I was 13, 14. We used to go down the Camden Palace, now KOKO. We used to go down there and try and get in. He was running the door then and I used to give him so much banter and he used to laugh. We used to turn up after the pubs. A lot of our friends would be in there. He'd see me coming. There'd be a queue down one side but I'd come from the other side, and he'd see me and I'd go, 'Alright, Lenny,' and depending how busy he was or whatever he'd just say, 'Go on, get in,' but if he had time he'd stand and listen to me giving him some banter. We were underage, but he knew some of us and he knew we were alright. We never caused no trouble in there and were all really good kids. If there was ever any trouble in there we would tell him. He was sweet.

VAS BLACKWOOD

Growing up in west London, knocking about, bunking off school and
staying out all night at clubs. You were going to come into contact
with Lenny McLean.

SIMON HAYES

Lenny McLean absolutely loved being involved with *Lock,
Stock and Two Smoking Barrels*. He had a lot of respect and love
for Guy and Matthew, and they did for him. It was this love
and respect that kept him working on the film even though
he was sick. Nobody knew except Guy and Matthew. Lenny
didn't want it to get out because, as he said:

I have a reputation as a fighter and if some people knew I was sick
and weak they would try to take me down. I'm a bit like an old Wild
West gunfighter. I'm the best at what I do and people want to be the
one that took Lenny McLean.

LENNY MCLEAN

Personally I doubt many people could have taken Lenny even
when he was sick. Any other person would have signed off
sick, but not Lenny McLean. He wasn't going to let a little
lung cancer get in his way or in the way of filming.

We didn't know he was ill, but he had this cough and he said, 'I can't
seem to shake this cough but I'll tell you what I'll do. I'll smash it.'
   We all looked at each other and asked what he meant.
   'I'm back on the training regime. There's only one thing to do
with bronchitis and that's road work. I'm gonna run it off. I'm up at
5 o'clock every morning doing me old boxing training.'
   Basically he tried to run off lung cancer.

SIMON HAYES

He had cancer while we were filming, but we had no clue. He was the consummate professional – more professional than a lot of actors. He turned up on time, knowing his lines, knowing exactly what he had to do.

TIM MAURICE-JONES

When he died there was a lot of people grieving. I was one, and I know Guy and Matthew were.

VAS BLACKWOOD

It was Matthew who made him go to the doctor. Like a lot of men, Lenny wasn't going to go to the doctor; he was going to run it off. Matthew came from a world where you did go to the doctor, and to hear this man coughing like he did and refusing to go to the doctor was completely foreign to him.

We all liked to take the piss out of Matthew because he was the guv'nor and he held the purse strings but he's a very, very caring man and a decent human being.

SIMON HAYES

Whenever I see movies I never buy the bad guys after meeting people like Lenny McLean, because, Lenny, all he wanted to do was have a laugh. Obviously he would do the business when he had to do the business, but most of the time all he wanted to do was tell funny stories. He was a hilarious man.

TIM MAURICE-JONES

Lenny was funny and he liked a laugh. I heard a story that demonstrates Lenny's humour. I don't know if it's true but it's a lovely story.

One day, at Three Mills in Bow, where the production offices were, Lenny came storming into the office demanding to see Matthew: 'Where's that producer? I want to speak to that fucking producer!'

Matthew was terrified and hiding in his office. A runner told him that Lenny was looking for him and that he was not going to leave until he had spoken with Matthew. Matthew had no choice – he had to come out of his office and face the furious man mountain. He nervously came out to find the entire office watching, wondering what had upset Lenny so much and what he was going to do. Matthew stood by his office door and looked at Lenny. Lenny looked him up and down, while Matt stood there shaking.

'Come here.'

'What?'

'Come here.'

'Lenny, whatever it is, I'm sure we can …'

'Shut up and come here.'

Matthew slowly and very reluctantly walked towards Lenny. When he got near Lenny he stopped.

'Closer.'

He took another step and Lenny reached out, grabbed him and gave him a huge hug, saying, 'I fucking love you.'

The whole room burst into laughter from the relief.

Lenny's Philosophy

In 1997, not long after the filming had finished, we all went to watch Vinnie play in a match for Wimbledon at Selhurst Park. Vinnie was fantastic. He had a private box laid on for all of us with all the trimmings – champagne, beer and buffet. Everybody was there, the cast, the producers, Guy, etc. The box was in a great position at the top of the stadium with an unblocked view of the pitch. When the game was on most people went outside on the terrace to watch the game, except for Lenny, myself and a few others who watched the game from inside through the window. Lenny said it was because he didn't like football. The reality was that Lenny's cancer was getting very bad at that time, and he was more comfortable sitting inside than standing on the windy, cold terrace.

Lenny loved to talk and be the centre of the party, and because he and I were the only ones who weren't watching the game closely he had my full attention to tell me loads of stories and share his philosophies. One of the philosophies he shared with me was about why he never lost his temper on the roads and why, if somebody cut him up or gestured at him, he wouldn't do anything about it. Even if he was furious inside he would keep himself calm and let it go. He said, 'The police know me and if I do anything they will come down on me. I'm not scared of that, or of getting banged up, but I've got my family to think of, Val and the kids. Me going inside over clumping somebody in a road rage incident isn't gonna help them.'

Quite how this next piece of Lenny McLean philosophy came out I don't remember. It may have been connected to the motoring philosophy:

'There are two types of people in this world. There's the type that, if you do anything to 'em, they will go to the law and grass you up and you're done. Or there's the type that will get their own back on you. They'll either come at you right there or they'll wait until you're not expecting it and they'll do you from behind.'

Then he went round the room pointing out people and telling me who he thought would go to the law and who would do him. When he came to me he took a long look at me and very pointedly said, 'You. You will wait and wait. You'll wait a long time but you'll get your own back on me. You'll wait until I'm not looking and you'll get me.'

He was right, I would have waited and waited a long time and then waited some more, and then I would have done nothing. After all, we're talking about the world champion bare-knuckle fighter, the man who took on the mafia and the IRA and won, Britain's Hardest Man. There aren't many people out there who would have taken him on. I have a feeling he was playing with me.

He would just tell you stories that were either hilarious or would make your toes curl and leave you thinking, 'I'm glad I'm not on the wrong side of him.'

TIM MAURICE-JONES

I asked Lenny about the audition one day when we were in a pub and he said to me, 'I don't audition, son. Watch this.' He pointed to a fella and mouthed the words, 'Come here, you cunt.' The geezer picked up his coat and walked out. 'You see, it's all acting, son.'

NICK MORAN

One of the runners, a posh friend of Matthew's, asked Lenny one day if he had gone to drama school. Lenny gave this 18-year-old posh kid a glance and said, 'Listen, son, I've been shot twice, stabbed six times and had hundreds of bar-room brawls. Isn't that enough drama for anyone?'

SIMON HAYES

This comment showed up Lenny's quick wit and intelligence; it was so endearing and so funny and was Lenny all over. And he wasn't lying either. He really had been shot twice, stabbed six times and had hundreds of bar room brawls.

Lenny McLean commanded respect without even trying. He could be in a room and you would know he was there. He was loud but not in an obnoxious way and you would often hear him before you saw him. You'd look round to see where the big laugh was coming from and be greeted by this 6ft 4in man mountain holding court and entertaining everybody. Lenny gave true meaning to the phrase 'he had hands like shovels'. I have never actually seen a man with hands his size and I would never have wanted to feel him punch me.

I didn't do any scenes with him. I mean, If Lenny asked me to go for a drink with him in his local boozer I'd be terrified. There was something slightly frightening about a boy like me talking to a Lenny McLean. I mean he probably loved his mum and all that but still. He turned up on set, I remember shaking this big hand and thinking, 'How many people have this hand punched?'

NICHOLAS ROWE

I worked with an actor once who had got punched by Lenny at Camden Palace in London. This actor got a little too drunk and fell through one of the fire doors, setting off the alarms. By the time he had picked himself of the floor, Lenny had run round from the front door and hit him with one punch and broken his jaw in four places. This may sound like Lenny was a thug, but in his defence he didn't know whether the alarm was set off by idiots trying to get in through the back door. Lenny was the kind of bloke to act first and ask questions later.

Lenny commanded respect from me on one occasion. The wrap party was at a club in Soho. When I arrived the party was in full swing. I saw Lenny and Vinnie sat at the bar deep in conversation. I went over to say hello, but Lenny just held up a finger and said, 'Wait!' Respect and a very large finger kept me quiet. After a short while they finished the conversation and both said hello.

P.H. was a chap in his younger days, a face. Actually he still is. When I met with him to talk about the book he was constantly being stopped for a chat by people who knew him. He also kept telling me stories and then he'd say, 'But you can't put that in the book.' He knew Lenny long before the film – he first came across him when they were both young fighters.

I used to train in a gym in Greenwich, top of Trafalgar Rd with junction of Blackwall Lane. It's all changed now, this was years ago. He was training, young guy, he was powerful then. I don't know if you've ever held a punch bag. Even with 11-year-olds you can feel it coming through the bag. He hit the bag and I said, 'Did you hit it? I've seen women put their make-up on harder than that with a

powder puff.' He put one into it, I swear to God it came through the bag and into my chest, I didn't half feel it. And I felt the power of his punches. I went, 'Give me a minute, Len, I need the toilet.' And I gave it the swerve. I came back but I had to get out of that, I mean he was so powerful. I've seen guys work the doors in gyms and I've seen them hit the bags, and if they hit somebody they'd kill 'em. But if you know how to punch correctly you get more out of it. Some people are natural punchers.

P.H. MORIARTY

Jason Flemyng had to share a three-way with him one day:

They're tiny and there's no way you can get two people in there, never mind Lenny and someone else. Matt Vaughn thought it would be really funny to tell Lenny I was gay.

'I've heard about you and I've got to say I'm a little bit disappointed.'

'No, no, Len, it's Matt Vaughn's little joke. It's not funny, it's just silly, I'm not gay.'

And he's like, ' You got to do what you got to do, son.'

He just couldn't get it out of his head. So I had this little rucksack and I'm a big Elvis fan. In this rucksack was an imported CD from Japan. It was an Elvis live concert rare CD that was only released in Japan, a really cool little thing. So I'd left it out on the side and I'd said to Lenny, I'll get changed outside in the rain and he was like, 'Good boy, good boy.'

When I came back in he was holding the CD and he said, 'What's this, boy?'

'It's an illegal recording of an Elvis gig from Japan.'

'That's good that is. Where d'ya get it from?'

'Well, they're hard to get.'

'Where can I get one from?'

And I went, 'you can have that one Lenny.'

And he went, 'Good boy, good boy.'

JASON FLEMYNG

He was an odd character, so many different things. He was an incredibly violent man, in his past, there's no getting away from it. He was. I think he knew how to separate his violent life from his normal life. He was a family man and he had a great relationship with his son, Jamie, but he was an unbelievably tough, violent man. It was like there was always two people in there.

We did the scene where I'm the guy being drowned in the bucket. When we did that scene I was nervous that he was going to kill me. We get there, cameras rolling, and he wouldn't hold my head under, I had to hold my head under. I came up and I said:

'Lenny, you have to hold my head under, I have to look like I'm struggling but if I struggle I'm going to pop up.'

He said, 'I don't want to hurt you.'

'It's ok. Push me a bit harder.'

We go again and I get to the end, I struggle and I pop out again. I said, 'Lenny, you've got to hold me under.'

'But I don't want to hurt you.'

'You've got to do it harder.'

So the next take he held me harder but it was still soft. He knew when to separate it.

He was photographically one of the best faces I've ever photographed. You put a light on him from any angle and photograph him, he looks amazing. Some people have a screen presence. You look at Brad Pitt or Robert Downey Jr through the lens and you can see you've got someone. You look at Lenny through the lens and you know, 'I've got someone.' If he hadn't died, people would have been lining up round the block to use him.

He scared the life out of my camera assistant. We had a shot that was slightly out of focus and Lenny called him over and sat him down and squeezed his leg really hard. 'What's this I hear about my shot being out of focus?'

The poor focus puller nearly fainted.

He just said, 'Alright son, off you go.'

TIM MAURICE-JONES

There was an air of authenticity on set with people like Lenny McLean, who was a kind of daunting figure of a person who was actually incredibly, fantastically polite and gentle – he was very, very sweet. There were a lot of characters around who gave it this sense of authenticity and I think that was a masterstroke from Guy because you felt the real thing was there, it was present. The Vinnie Jones thing was a masterstroke because he was so charismatic. He was great. It worked. I didn't have any scenes with Lenny, but I remember meeting him by the catering truck and having this man mountain towering over me. He was delightful and very warm and generous. Not someone you'd easily forget.

STEVEN MACKINTOSH

The Guv'nor. April 1949–July 1998.

'it's been emotional'

Big Chris.

While I've been writing this book, searching online etc. I've come across some of the most important people who made *Lock, Stock and Two Smoking Barrels* a success – the fans. Some of the fans have expressed their love for the film in various

Banknotes by www.maxjake.com @maxjakeadvertising.

unusual ways from playing drinking games while quoting the dialogue of the film to fancy-dress pub crawls dressed as their favourite characters. Some people have gone to more extremes, as the photographs in this chapter show.

Steven Mackintosh's daughter is at university with some guys on a marketing/advertising course and they had to come up with an interesting marketing strategy. They made up

banknotes with images of the *Lock, Stock* characters on them and a couple of fake Twitter accounts for Rory Breaker and Hatchett Harry.

Vas shared a picture with me that someone had shared on Facebook of his image on the side of a truck. I tracked the truck owner down – his name is Chris Bultitude of Shifty Haulage. I drove to meet him at his yard in Felixstowe and got some great pictures of his truck. He and his brothers absolutely loved the film and Guy's follow-up film, *Snatch*. Chris is thinking of getting another truck one day and he's going to paint that with characters from *Snatch*.

From one big truck to a very small car.

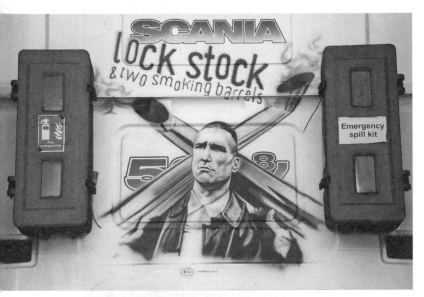

A Corgi figurine and car that can be found on Amazon for $65.

Lock, Stock **tattoos.**

The weirdest things I've found are tattoos that are influenced by the film – only three of them, but they're very strong tattoos.

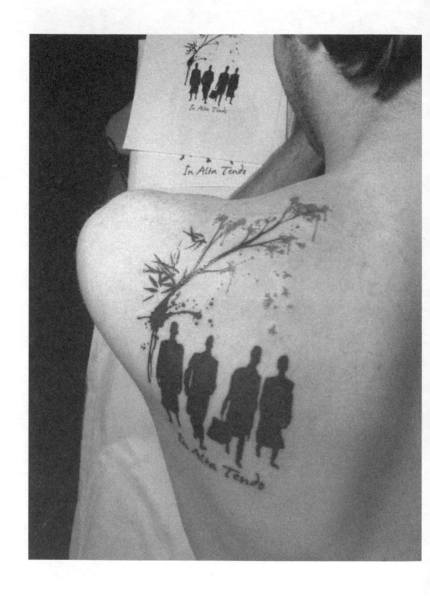

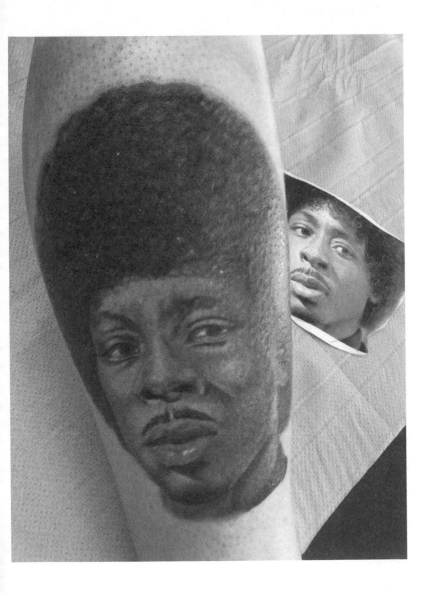

The Players

To close the book I thought it might be of interest to give you a brief biography and 'where are they now?' of some of the main players:

guy ritchie was born on 10 September 1968 in Hatfield, Hertfordshire. He was the second of two kids born to Amber and Captain John Vivian Ritchie. Guy was expelled from Stanbridge Earls School at the age of 15. He has said that drug use was the reason for the expulsion; his dad said it was because his son was caught 'cutting class and entertaining a girl in his room'. I bet it was both.

Guy has gone on to make loads of other films as director, writer and producer. They've included *Snatch* (Director/Writer), *RocknRolla* (Director/Producer/Writer), *Sherlock Holmes* (Director), *Man From Uncle* (Director/Producer/Writer) and *King Arthur: Legend of The Sword* (Director/Writer Producer). Guy is currently writing *Sherlock Holmes 3* and working on a live-action version of *Aladdin* for Disney.

matthew vaughn was born on 7 March 1971 in London. Matt went to Stowe School in Buckingham. He dropped out of University College London after only a few weeks and took a gap year. He began film making and produced a film starring Michael Gambon called *The Innocent Sleep* in 1995. It was after this that he met Guy and they dropped everything to work on *Lock, Stock*. Since the success of *Lock, Stock* he has produced *Snatch*, *Mean Machine* and *Swept Away* with Guy under the Ska Films banner. Guy and Matthew have since split, and Matthew has directed and produced many films since including *Layer Cake* (Director), *Kick Ass* (Director), *X-Men: Days of Future Past* (Writer) and *X-Men: First Class* (Director/Writer), *Kingsman* (Director/Producer/Writer), *Fantastic Four* (Producer) and *Eddie the Eagle* (Producer), directed by Dexter Fletcher.

trudie styler was born on 6 January 1954. She is an English film producer and director. She got involved with *Lock, Stock and Two Smoking Barrels* when Guy and Matthew brought her the script. She liked it and she had seen Guy's short film and based on those two things she agreed to invest in it and became an executive producer. She has executive produced numerous films both before and since *Lock, Stock*.

nick moran was born on 23 December 1969 in London's East End. He grew up just outside Watford on the South Oxhey council estate. He is married to Dr Jasmin Duran and was previously married to actress Sienna Guillory.

Before *Lock, Stock*, Nick and I worked together on a little video called *Drinking Games*. The title says it all – it's instructions on how to play all those drunk games one plays at parties. I presented it and Nick was one of the actors demonstrating the rules, which meant that he and three others would re-enact how to play the games. One day he was very hungover from the night before and we were filming on a boat on the Thames, and despite using non-alcoholic lager he spent a lot of the day heaving over the side of the boat. Who knew that we would work together a few months later on one of the biggest British movies in years?

After *Lock, Stock* Nick was voted *GQ* man of the year. I wonder if he'd have got that vote if they'd seen him on that boat.

Nick is front man for his own Frank Sinatra tribute band. He still acts and has been seen in *Harry Potter and The Deathly Hallows*, *St George's Day* (directed by Frank Harper) and *Prisoners of the Sun*. He can be seen in *Eat Locals* (Jason Flemyng's directing debut) and *My Name is Lenny*. He is also a director, writer and producer. His films have included *Telstar: The Joe Meek Story*, *Baby Juice Express* (I played a role in that) and *The Kid*.

Jason Statham was born on 26 July 1967 in Derbyshire, before his family moved to Great Yarmouth. He was always athletic and is a very accomplished martial artist. He was also a diver for Great Britain and competed in the Commonwealth Games. While training at Crystal Palace pool he was spotted by a sports modelling agency and became the face of French Connection.

After *Lock, Stock* Jason did *Snatch* alongside Brad Pitt and this opened up Hollywood for him. He's since starred in many films including the *Transporter* series, *Crank*, *The Italian Job*, *Revolver*, *In the Name of the King*, *The Bank Job*, *The Expendables* and some of the *Fast and Furious* films.

jason flemyng was born on 25 September 1966 in Putney. His dad was a TV and film director known for directing TV shows like *Lovejoy* and *Taggart* and two classic *Doctor Who* movies, *Doctor Who and The Daleks* and *Daleks, Invasion Earth*.

His first TV appearance was in 1991 in *Rich Tea and Sympathy*. In 1996 he played the lead in a movie called *Alive and Kicking* opposite Anthony Sher. This brought him to the attention of the business and he found himself, in 1997, working with the Spice Girls in *Spice World*. Then came *Lock, Stock*. Since then he's developed a skill of 'being slightly out of focus behind really expensive actors',[1] such as Sean Connery in *League of Extraordinary Gentlemen*, and Brad Pitt in *Snatch* and *The Curious Case of Benjamin Button*. He's also worked with *Lock, Stock* buddies Dexter Fletcher in *Sunshine on Leith* and *Wild Bill*, Jason Statham in *Transporter 2* and Matthew Vaughn in *X-Men: First Class*.

Jason is currently on TV in *SS-GB* and can be seen in the upcoming film *Journey to China: Mystery of Iron Mask*, produced by Jackie Chan. He has also started directing – last year he directed a film called *Eat Locals*. He reunited the four boys from *Lock, Stock* for it, but they're not all on screen – Dexter and Nick are, but Jason Statham did the fight arranging.

---

1   http://www.telegraph.co.uk/culture/tvandradio/5017193/Jason-Flemyng-on-starring-in-Primeval-Interview.html

dexter fletcher was born on 31 January 1966 in Enfield, London. Dexter's acting career started very early in his life when he played Baby Face in Alan Parker's *Bugsy Malone*. He has never stopped working and seems to have been in everything, from *Press Gang*, *Hotel Babylon*, *The Long Good Friday* and *The Elephant Man* to the HBO series *Band of Brothers*. He has also directed films, debuting with *Wild Bill*, followed by *Sunshine on Leith* and most recently *Eddie the Eagle*.

vinnie jones was born on 5 January 1965 in Watford. His acting career began with the part of Big Chris in *Lock, Stock*. Guy saw Vinnie do a walk-on part and just offered him the role from that. After *Snatch* came up and the role of Bullet Tooth Tony, Vinnie went to Hollywood, generally playing himself, but doing it very well. He's been in films with John Travolta (*Swordfish*), Nicholas Cage and Angelina Jolie (*Gone in Sixty Seconds*) and, of course, Brad Pitt (*Snatch*). His Hollywood career has really taken off and he lives out there now.

p.h. moriarty was born in 1939 and lives in Sevenoaks in Kent. P.H. has worked on several of the greatest British gangster films ever made, starting in 1979 with *Quadrophenia*, followed by *Scum*, and then in 1980 he played Razors in one of my favourite movies *The Long Good Friday*, which also introduced Pierce Brosnan to the world. Then a few turkeys, including *Jaws 3-D*, until *Lock, Stock and Two Smoking Barrels*.

lenny mcLean was born in 1949 in Hoxton, East London. Lenny only acted professionally for two years. He began in 1996 in *The Knock* as smuggler Eddie Davies and then had a small part in *The Fifth Element* before finally playing Barry The Baptist. He wasn't known for his acting but he gave such a powerful performance in *Lock, Stock*, despite being very sick, that one can't forget him.

steven mackintosh was born in Cambridge on 30 April 1967. Steven is a very talented and versatile actor and is known for a lot of varied roles, including Winston in *Lock, Stock*, of course, the posh drug dealer. He's also played a vampire in the *Underworld* series of films, a cop in *Luther* and a robber in *Inside Men*. He's been in *The Sweeney*, *Kick Ass 2* and *Blue Juice*, and he can currently be seen in the TV series *The Halcyon*.

Vas blackwood was born on 17 January 1962 in St Pancras, London. His full name is Vasta R. Blackwood but everyone calls him Vas. His acting career started in 1981 but he first got noticed by the public in one episode of *Only Fools and Horses* playing the funny bank robber Lennox Gilbey ('The Shaaa aaa Dow') and then as Lenny Henry's side kick Winston in *The Lenny Henry Show*. This was followed by three series of 'Spatz', playing Dexter, the manager of a fast-food restaurant, and numerous other TV and film appearances.

We've just shot a film together, *Fanged Up*, a comedy about vampires in a prison.

index